Machine Learning for Beginners:

Step-by-Step Guide to Machine Learning, a Beginners Approach to Artificial Intelligence, Big Data, Basic Python Algorithms, and Techniques for Business (Practical Examples)

Copyright and Liability Disclaimer

2

Table of Contents

3

Conclusion

Introduction

Congratulations on purchasing **Machine Learning for Beginners:** Step-by-Step Guide to Machine Learning, a Beginners Approach to Artificial Intelligence, Big Data, Basic Python Algorithms and Techniques for Business (Practical Examples) and thank you for doing so.

The following chapters will address the key concepts of machine learning algorithms and the need for machine learning to solve contemporary business problems. In the first chapter of this book, you'll be given a comprehensive explanation about the importance of machine learning algorithms and various machine learning libraries available on the market today. You will also learn about a variety of frequently used terms and the three core concepts in the realm of machine learning.

In Chapter 2 of this book titled, "Machine Learning Algorithms," you will learn the development and application of some of the most popular supervised machine learning algorithms, with explicit details on regression and decision trees. You will also learn some of the prominent unsupervised machine learning algorithms, including clustering and dimensionality reduction.

Chapter 3, titled "Fundamentals and Importance of Artificial Intelligence," will provide overarching guidance for everything you need to know about Artificial Intelligence. As business leaders of tomorrow, you will learn the importance and wide variety of applications of Artificial Intelligence technology in every aspect of our digital life. You will also learn the advantages and disadvantages of Artificial Intelligence technology in every existing industrial domain.

The final chapter of this book will be titled "Web Marketing." You will get an overview of the marketing applications of AI technology with AI-based instruments such as "GetResponse Autofunnel," which have automated the traditional method of generating industry-specific and business-specific marketing funnels to attract prospective clients and transform them into paying customers. As a business leader, you need to keep up to date on tools and technologies that can help you grow and expand your business, and as you learn with this book, the future lies within the scope of state-of-the-art technologies such as AI, Machine Learning and Big Data Analysis. Therefore, we have also delivered a thorough explanation of what big data is and how contemporary analytical instruments and techniques can be applied to this data treasure to obtain valuable insights and bring your company to the next level, in the 4th chapter of this book titled, "Big Data Analytics 101".

This highly technical subject has been carefully crafted to cater specifically to business-oriented individuals with a non-technical background. You will find abundant real-life examples to help you gain a total understanding of the topics discussed. Special efforts have been made to explain the technical jargon in simple colloquial language.

There are plenty of books on this subject on the market, thanks again for choosing this one! Every effort was made to ensure it is full of as much useful information as possible. Please enjoy!

Chapter 1: Introduction to Machine Learning

The notion of Artificial Intelligence Technology is derived from the idea that computers can be engineered to exhibit human-like intelligence and mimic human reasoning and learning capacities, adapting to fresh inputs and performing duties without needing human intervention. The principle of artificial intelligence encompasses machine learning. Machine Learning Technology (ML) refers to the principle of Artificial Intelligence Technology, which focuses mainly on the designed ability of computers to learn explicitly and self-train, identifying information patterns to enhance the underlying algorithm and making autonomous decisions without human involvement. In 1959, the term "machine learning" was coined during his tenure at IBM, by the pioneering gaming and artificial intelligence professor, Arthur Samuel.

Machine learning hypothesizes that contemporary computers can be trained using targeted training data sets, which can readily be tailored to create required functionality. Machine learning is guided by a pattern recognition method where previous interactions and outcomes are recorded and revisited in a way that corresponds to its present position. Because machines are needed to process infinite volumes of data, with fresh data constantly flowing in, they need to be equipped to adapt to the fresh data without being programmed by a person, considering the iterative aspect of machine learning. Machine learning has close relations with the field of Statistics, which is focused on generating predictions using advanced computing tools and technologies. The research of "mathematical optimization" provides the field of machine learning with techniques, theories, and implementation areas. Machine learning is also referred to as "predictive analytics" in its implementation to address business issues. In ML the "target" is known as "label" while in statistics it's called "dependent variable". A "variable" in statistics is known as "feature" in ML. And a "feature creation" in ML is known as "transformation" in statistics.

ML technology is also closely related to data mining and optimization. ML and data mining often utilize the same techniques with considerable overlap. ML focuses on generating predictions on the basis of predefined characteristics of the given training data. On the other hand, data mining pertains to the identification of unknown characteristics in a large volume of data. Data mining utilizes many techniques of ML, but with distinct objectives; similarly, machine learning also uses techniques of data mining through the "unsupervised learning algorithms" or as a pre-processing phase to enhance the prediction accuracy of the model. The intersection of these two distinct research areas stems from the fundamental assumptions with which they operate. In machine learning, efficiency is generally assessed with regard to the capacity of the model to reproduce known knowledge, while in "knowledge discovery and information mining (KDD)" the main job is to discover new information. An "uninformed or unsupervised" technique, evaluated in terms of known information, will be easily outperformed by other "supervised techniques." On the contrary, "supervised techniques" cannot be used in a typical "KDD" task owing to the lack of training data.

Data optimization is another area that machine learning is closely linked with. Various learning issues can be formulated as minimization of certain "loss function" on the training data set. "Loss functions" are derived as the difference between the predictions generated by the model being trained and the input data values The distinction between the two areas stems from the objective of "generalization". Optimization algorithms are designed to decrease the loss on the training data set; the objective of machine learning is to minimize the loss of input data from the real world.

Machine learning has become such a "heated" issue that its definition varies across the world of academia, corporate companies, and the scientific community. Here are some of the commonly accepted definitions from select sources that are extremely known:

- "Machine learning is based on algorithms that can learn from data without relying on rules-based programming." – McKinsey.
- "Machine Learning at its most basic is the practice of using algorithms to parse data, learn from it, and then make a determination or prediction about something in the world." – Nvidia
- "The field of Machine Learning seeks to answer the question, how can we build computer systems that automatically improve with experience, and what are the fundamental laws that govern all learning processes?" – Carnegie Mellon University
- "Machine learning is the science of getting computers to act without being explicitly programmed." – Stanford University

Core Concepts of Machine Learning

Today there are several kinds of ML, but the notion of ML is mainly based on three components "representation", "evaluation" and "optimization". Here are some of the standard concepts that are applicable to all of them:

Representation

Machine learning models can not directly hear, see or sense input examples. Data representation is therefore needed to provide a helpful vantage point for the model in the main data attributes. The choice of significant characteristics that best represent data is very essential to train a machine learning model effectively. "Representation" simply refers to the act of "representing" data points to computer in a language that it understands using a set of classifiers. A classifier may be defined as "a model that inputs a vector of discrete and/or ongoing function values and outputs a single discrete value called "class". To learn from the represented data, a model must have the desired classifier in the training data set or "hypothesis space"

18

that you want the models to be trained on. The data features used to represent the input are very critical to the machine learning system. Any "classifier" that is external to the hypothesis space cannot be learned by the model. For developing a required machine learning model, data characteristics are so essential that it can easily be the difference between successful and unsuccessful machine learning projects.

A training data set with several independent "features" which are well linked to the "class" can make learning much easier for the machine. On the other side, it may not be easy for the machine to learn from the class with complex functions. This often requires processing of the raw data so that the desired features for the ML model can be built from it. The method of deriving features from raw data set tends to be the ML project's most time-consuming and laborious component. It is also considered to be the most creative and interesting part of the project where intuition and "trial and error" play just as important a role as the technical requirements. The ML process is not a "one shot" process of developing and executing a training data set, but an iterative process requiring analysis of the post-execution output, followed by modification of the training data set. Domain specificity is another reason why the training dataset requires comprehensive time and effort. Training data set to produce predictions based on consumer behavior analysis for an e-commerce platform will be very distinct from the training data set needed to create a self-driving car.

Nevertheless, in the industrial sectors the core machine learning mechanism stays the same. No wonder, there is a lot of research going on to automate the process of feature engineering.

Evaluation

Essentially, in context of ML "evaluation" is referred to as the method of assessing various hypotheses or models to select one model over another. A "evaluation function" is needed to distinguish between effective classifiers from the vague ones. The evaluation function is also known as the "objective," "utility," or "scoring" function. The machine learning algorithm has its own internal evaluation function that is usually very different from the researchers ' external evaluation function used to optimize the classifier. Usually the evaluation function is described as the first phase of the project before selecting the data representation tool. For example, the self-driving car machine learning model has the feature to identify pedestrians in its vicinity at near zero false negative and low false positive rate as an "evaluation function" and the pre-existing condition that needs to be "represented" using applicable data features.

Optimization

The process of searching the hypothesis space of the represented machine learning model to identify the highest scoring classifier and achieve better evaluation is called "optimization." For algorithms with more than one optimum classifier, selecting the optimization method is very critical in determining the generated classifier and achieving a more effective model of learning. There are a variety of "off-the-shelf optimizers" on the market to kick off new machine learning models before replacing them with custom designed optimizers.

Frequently Used Machine Learning Terminologies and Their Definitions

Agent – In the context of reinforcement learning, an agent refers to "the entity that uses a policy to maximize expected return gained from transitioning between states of the environment."

Boosting – Boosting can be defined as "a machine learning technique that iteratively combines a set of simple and not very accurate classifiers (referred to as weak classifiers) into a classifier with high accuracy (a strong classifier) by up-weighting the examples that the model is currently misclassifying."

Candidate Generation – The phase of selecting the "first set of recommendations" by a recommendation system is referred to as candidate generation. For example, "Amazon Kindle" can offer a million different book titles to the customer. The candidate generation technique can be used to produce a subset of few 1000 books meeting the needs of a particular user and can be easily refined further to an even smaller set as needed.

Categorical Data – Data features boasting a "discrete set of possible values" is called categorical data, such as a "categorical feature" labeled automobile style can have an unconnected set of multiple possible values including truck, coupe, minivan and so on.

Checkpoint – Checkpoint can be defined as "The data that can capture the state of the variables of a learning model particular moment in time." With the use of checkpoints, training can be carried out across multiple sessions, and model weights or scores can be exported.

Class – Class can be defined as "one of a set of listed target values for a given label." For example, a machine learning model designed to detect "spam" will have two classes, namely, "spam" and "not spam".

Classification model – The type of ML model used to "distinguish between two or more discrete classes of data" is referred to as a classification model. For example, a classification model for identification of shoes could assess whether the shoe picture used as input is sneakers, pumps, sandals, wedges, boots, and so on.

Collaborative filtering – "The process of generating predictions for a particular user based on the shared interests of a group of similar users" is called collaborative filtering.

Continuous feature – It is defined as a "floating-point feature with an infinite range of possible values".

Discrete feature – It is defined as a "rigid feature with a finite set of possible values."

Discriminator – "The system that determines whether the input examples are real or fake" is called as a discriminator.

Down-sampling – The process of Down-sampling refers to "the act of reducing the amount of information contained in a feature or using a disproportionately low percentage of over-represented class examples in order to train the learning model more efficiently."

Dynamic model – "A learning model that is continuously receiving input data to be trained in a continuous manner" is called a dynamic model.

Ensemble – "The set of predictions generated by merging predictions of multiple models" is called as an ensemble.

Environment – The term "environment" used in the context of reinforcement machine learning constitutes "the world that contains the agent and allows the agent to observe that world's state".

Episode – The term episode used in context of reinforcement machine learning constitutes "every iterative attempt made by the agent to learn from its environment".

Feature – "An input data variable that is used in generating predictions" is called as a feature.

Feature engineering – Feature engineering can be defined as "the process of determining which features might be useful in training a model, and then converting raw data from log files and other sources into said features".

Feature extraction – Feature extraction can be defined as "the process of Retrieving intermediate feature representations calculated by an unsupervised or pre-trained model for use in another model as input".

Few-shot learning - Few-shot learning can be defined as "a machine learning approach, often used for object classification, designed to learn effective classifiers from only a small number of training examples".

Fine tuning – The process of "performing a secondary optimization to adjust the parameters of an already trained model to fit a new problem" is called as fine tuning. It is widely used to refit the weights of a "trained unsupervised model" to a "supervised model".

Generalization – "The ability of the machine learning model to make correct predictions on new, previously unseen data as opposed to the data used to train the model" is called as generalization.

Inference – In context of ML, inference can be defined as "the process of making predictions by applying the trained model to unlabeled examples".

Label – In context of machine learning (supervised), the "answer" or "result" part of an example is called as label. A labeled data set can constitute single or multiple features and corresponding labels for every example. For example, in a country related data set, the "features" could include the name of the city, population of the city, while the label can be the "country name".

Linear model – Linear model is defined as "a model that assigns one weight per feature to make predictions".

Loss – In the context of machine learning, loss refers to the "measure of how far are the predictions generated by the model from its label."

Matplotlib – It is "an open-source Python 2D plotting library which is used to visualize different aspects of machine learning".

Model – In the context of ML, a model can be defined as "the representation of what a machine learning system has learned from the training data."

NumPy – "An open-source math library that provides efficient array operations in Python".

One-shot learning – In the context of ML, one-shot learning refers to "a machine learning approach designed to learn effective classifiers from a single training example, often used for object classification."

Overfitting - In the context of machine learning, overfitting is referred to as "creation of a model that matches the training data so closely that the model fails to make correct predictions on new data."

Parameter – "A variable of a model that the machine learning system is able to train on its own" is called as a parameter.

Pipeline – In the context of ML, pipeline refers to "the infrastructure surrounding a machine learning algorithm and includes a collection of data, addition of the data to training data files, training one or more models, and exporting the models to production."

Random forest – In the context of machine learning, the concept of random forest pertains to "an ensemble approach for finding the decision tree that best fits the training data by developing multiple decision trees with a random selection of features."

Scaling - In the context of machine learning, scaling refers to "a common feature engineering practice to tame a feature's range of values to match the range of other features in the dataset."

Under-fitting - In the context of ML, under-fitting refers to "production of an ML model with poor predictive ability because the model hasn't captured the complexity of the training data."

Validation – "The process used to evaluate the quality of a machine learning model using the validation set, as part of the model training phase" is called validation. The primary purpose of this process is to make sure that the performance of the ML model can be applied beyond the training set.

Machine Learning in Practice

The complete process of machine learning is much more extensive than just the development and application of machine learning algorithms and can be divided into steps below:

1. Define the goals of the project, taking into careful consideration all the prior knowledge and domain expertise available. Goals can quickly become ambiguous since there are always new things you want to achieve than practically possible to implement.

2. The data pre-processing and cleaning must result in a high-quality data set. This is the most critical and time-consuming step of the whole project. The larger the volume of data, the more noise it brings to the training data set which must be eradicated before feeding to the learner system.

3. Selection of appropriate learning model to meet the requirements of your project. This process tends to be rather simple, given the various types of data models available in the market.

4. Depending on the domain the machine learning model is applied to, the results may or may not require a clear understanding of the model by human experts as long as the model can successfully deliver desired results.

5. The final step is to consolidate and deploy the knowledge or information gathered from the model to be used on an industrial level.

6. The whole cycle from step 1 to 5 listed above is iteratively repeated until a result that can be used in practice is achieved.

Importance of Machine Learning

The seemingly unstoppable interest in ML stems from the same variables that have made "data mining" and "Bayesian analysis" more common than ever before. The underlying factors contributing to this popularity are increasing quantities and data varieties, cheaper and more effective computational processing, and inexpensive data storage. To get a sense of how significant machine learning is in our everyday lives, it is simpler to state what part of our cutting edge way of life has not been touched by it. Each aspect of human life is being impacted by the "smart machines" intended to expand human capacities and improve efficiencies. Artificial Intelligence and machine learning technology is the focal precept of the "Fourth Industrial Revolution", that could possibly question our thoughts regarding being "human."

"Google's self-driving cars and robots get a lot of press, but the company's real future is in machine learning, the technology that enables computers to get smarter and more personal."
– Eric Schmidt, Google

All of these factors imply that models that can analyze larger, more complicated data while delivering highly accurate results in a short period of time can be produced rapidly and automatically on a much larger scale. Companies can easily identify potential growth opportunities or avoid unknown hazards by constructing desired machine learning models that meet their business requirements. Data runs through the vein of every company. Increasingly, data-driven strategies create a distinction between winning or losing the competition. Machine learning offers the magic of unlocking the importance of business and customer data to lead to actionable measures and decisions that can skyrocket a company's business and market share.

Machine learning has demonstrated over recent years that many distinct tasks can be automated which were once deemed as activities only people could carry out, such as image recognition, text processing, and gaming.

In 2014, Machine Learning and AI professionals believed the board game "Go" would take at least ten years for the machine to defeat its greatest player in the world. But they were proved mistaken by "Google's

DeepMind," which showed that machines are capable of learning which moves to take into account even in such a complicated game as "Go." In the world of gaming, machines have seen much more innovations such as "Dota Bot" from the "OpenAI" team. Machine learning is bound to have enormous economic and social impacts on our day to day lives. A complete set of work activities and the entire industrial spectrum could potentially be automated, and the labor market will be transformed forever.

"Machine learning is a method of data analysis that automates analytical model building. It is a branch of artificial intelligence based on the idea that systems can learn from data, identify patterns, and make decisions with minimal human intervention."
- SAS

Repetitive learning automation and information revelation. Unlike robotic automation driven by hardware that merely automates manual tasks, machine learning continuously and reliably enables the execution of high quantity, high volume, and computer-oriented tasks. Artificial intelligence machine learning algorithms help to adapt to the changing landscape by enabling a machine or system to learn, to take note of, and to reduce its previous mistakes. The machine learning algorithm works as a classifier or a forecasting tool to develop unique abilities and to define data patterns and structure. For instance, an algorithm for machine learning has created a model that will teach itself how to play chess and even how to generate product suggestions based on consumer activity and behavioral data. This model is so effective because it can easily adjust to any new data set.

Machine learning allows the assessment of more profound and wider data sets by means of neural networks comprising several hidden layers. Just a couple of years ago, a scheme for detecting fraud with countless hidden layers would have been considered a work of imagination. A whole new world is on the horizon with the emergence of big data and unimaginable computer capabilities. The data on the machines is like the gas on the vehicle—more data addition leads to faster and more accurate results. Deep learning models thrive with a wealth of data because they benefit from the information immediately. The machine-learning algorithms have led to incredible accuracy through the« deep neural networks.» Increased accuracy is obtained from deep learning, for instance, from the regular and extensive use of smart technology such as "Amazon Alexa" and "Google Search." These "deep neural networks" also boost our healthcare sector. Technologies like image classification and the recognition of objects are now able to detect cancer with the same precision as a heavily qualified radiologist on MRIs.

Artificial intelligence enables the use of big data analytics in combination with an algorithm for machine learning to be enhanced and improved. Data has developed like its own currency and can readily become "intellectual property" when algorithms are self-learning. The crude information is comparable to a goldmine in that the more and more you dig, the more you can dig out or extract "gold" or meaningful insights. The use of machine learning algorithms for the data allows faster discovery of the appropriate solutions and can make these solutions more useful. Bear in mind that the finest data will always be the winner, even though everyone uses similar techniques.

"Humans can typically create one or two good models a week; machine learning can create thousands of models a week."
- Thomas Davenport, The Wall Street Journal

Machine Learning Libraries

Machine learning libraries are sensitive routines and functions that are written in any given language. Software developers require a robust set of libraries to perform complex tasks without needing to rewrite multiple lines of code. Machine learning is largely based upon mathematical optimization, probability, and statistics.

Python is the language of choice in the field of machine learning credited to consistent development time and flexibility. It is well suited to develop sophisticated models and production engines that can be directly plugged into production systems. One of its greatest assets is an extensive set of libraries that can help researchers who are less equipped with developer knowledge to execute machine learning easily.

Scikit-Learn

"Scikit-Learn" has evolved as the gold standard for machine learning using Python, offering a wide variety of "supervised" and "unsupervised" ML algorithms. It is touted as one of the most user-friendly and cleanest machine learning libraries to date—for example, decision trees, clustering, linear and logistics regressions and K-means. Scikit-learn uses a couple of basic Python libraries: NumPy and SciPy and adds a set of algorithms for data mining tasks including classification, regression, and clustering. It is also capable ofimplementing tasks like feature selection, transforming data, and ensemble methods in only a few lines.

In 2007, David Cournapeau developed the foundational code of "Scikit-Learn" as part of a "Summer of Code" project for "Google." Scikit-learn has become one of Python's most famous open-source machine learning libraries since its launch in 2007. But it wasn't until 2010 that Scikit-Learn was released for public use. Scikit-Learn is an open-sourced, and BSD licensed, data mining and data analysis tool used to develop supervise and unsupervised machine learning algorithms build on Python. Scikit-learn offers various ML algorithms such as "classification," "regression," "dimensionality reduction," and "clustering." It also offers modules for feature extraction, data processing, and model evaluation.

Designed as an extension to the "SciPy" library, Scikit-Learn is based on "NumPy" and "matplotlib", the most popular Python libraries. NumPy expands Python to support efficient operations on big arrays and multidimensional matrices. Matplotlib offers visualization tools, and science computing modules are provided by SciPy. For scholarly studies, Scikit-Learn is popular because it has a well-documented, easy-to-use, and flexible API. Developers are able to utilize Scikit-Learn for their experiments with various algorithms by only altering a few lines of the code. Scikit-Learn also provides a variety of training datasets, enabling developers to focus on algorithms instead of data collection and cleaning. Many of the algorithms of Scikit-Learn are quick and scalable to all but huge datasets. Scikit-learn is known for its reliability, and automated tests are available for much of the library. Scikit-learn is extremely popular with beginners in machine learning to start implementing simple algorithms.

Prerequisites for Application of Scikit-Learn Library

The "Scikit-Learn" library is based on the "SciPy (Scientific Python)," which needs to be installed before using "SciKit-Learn." This stack involves the following:

- **NumPy (Base n-dimensional array package)**

"NumPy" is the basic package with Python to perform scientific computations. It includes among other things: "a powerful N-dimensional array object; sophisticated (broadcasting) functions; tools for integrating C/C++ and Fortran code; useful linear algebra, Fourier transform, and random number capabilities." NumPy is widely reckoned as an effective multi-dimensional container of generic data in addition to its apparent scientific uses. It is possible to define arbitrary data types. This enables NumPy to integrate with a wide variety of databases seamlessly and quickly. The primary objective of NumPy is the homogeneity of the multidimensional array. It consists of an element table (generally numbers), all of which are of the same sort and are indicated by tuples of non-negative integers. The dimensions of NumPy are called "axes" and array class is called "ndarray."

- **Matplotlib (Comprehensive 2D/3D plotting)**

"Matplotlib" is a 2-dimensional graphic generation library from Python that produces high-quality numbers across a range of hardcopy formats and interactive environments. The "Python script," the "Python," "IPython shells," the "Jupyter notebook," the web app servers, and select user interface toolkits can be used with matplottib. Matplotlib attempts to simplify easy tasks further and make difficult tasks feasible. With only a few lines of code, you can produce tracks, histograms, scatter plots, bar graphs, error graphs, etc.

A MATLAB-like interface is provided for easy plotting of the Pyplot Module, especially when coupled with

IPython. As a power user, you can regulate the entire line styles, fonts properties, and axis properties, through an object-oriented interface or through a collection of features similar to the one provided to MATLAB users.

Scipy (Fundamental Library for Scientific Computing)

SciPy is a "collection of mathematical algorithms and convenience functions built on the NumPy extension of Python," capable of adding more impact to interactive Python sessions, by offering high-level data manipulation and visualization commands and courses for the user. An interactive Python session with SciPy becomes an environment that rivals data processing and system prototyping technologies including "MATLAB, IDL, Octave, R-Lab, and SciLab."

Another advantage of developing "SciPy" on Python, is the accessibility of a strong programming language in the development of advanced programs and specific apps. Scientific apps using SciPy benefit from developers around theglobe, developing extra modules in countless software landscape niches. Everything produced has been made accessible to the Python programmer, from database subroutines and classes as well as "parallel programming to the web." These powerful tools are provided along with the "SciPy" mathematical libraries.

IPython (Enhanced interactive console)

"IPython (Interactive Python)" is an interface or command shell for interactive computing using a variety of programming languages. "IPython" was initially created exclusively for Python, which supports introspection, rich media, shell syntax, tab completion, and history. Some of the functionalities provided by IPython include: "interactive shells (terminal and Qt-based); browser-based notebook interface with code, text, math, inline plots and other media support; support for interactive data visualization and use of

GUI tool kits; flexible interpreters that can be embedded to load into your own projects; tools for parallel computing".

SymPy (Symbolic mathematics)

Developed by Ondřej Čertík and Aaron Meurer, SymPy is "an open-source Python library for symbolic computation." It offers algebra computing abilities to other apps, as a stand-alone app and/or as a library as well as live on the internet applications with "SymPy Live" or "SymPy Gamma." "SymPy" is easy to install and test, owing to the fact that it is completely developed in Python boasting limited dependencies. SymPy involves characteristics ranging from calculus, algebra, discrete mathematics, and quantum physics to fundamental symbolic arithmetic. The outcome of the computations can be formatted as "LaTeX" code. In combination with a straightforward, expandable codebase in a widespread programming language, the ease of access provided by SymPy makes it a computer algebra system with a comparatively low entry barrier.

Pandas (Data Structures and Analysis)

Pandas provide highly intuitive and user-friendly high-level data structures. Pandas has achieved popularity in the machine learning algorithm developer community, with built-in techniques for data aggregation, grouping, and filtering as well as results of time series analysis. The Pandas library has two primary structures: one-dimensional "Series" and two-dimensional "Data Frames."

Seaborn (Data Visualization)

Seaborn is derived from the Matplotlib Library and an extremely popular visualization library. It is a high-level library that can generate specific kinds of graphs, including heat maps, time series, and violin plots.

TensorFlow

TensorFlow can be defined as a Machine Learning platform providing end-to-end service with a variety of free and open sources. It has a system of multilayered nodes that allow for quick building, training, and deployment of artificial neural networks with large data sets. It is touted as a "simple and flexible architecture to take new ideas from concept to code to state-of-the-art models and to publication at a rapid pace." For example, Google uses TensorFlow libraries in its image recognition and speech recognition tools and technologies.

Higher-level APIs such as "tf.estimator" can be used for specifying predefined architectures, such as "linear regressors" or "neural networks." The picture below shows the existing hierarchy of the TensorFlow tool kit:

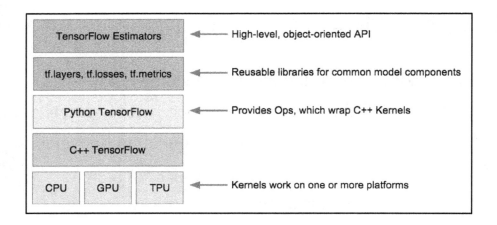

The picture shown below provides the purposes of the different layers:

Toolkit(s)	Description
Estimator (tf.estimator)	High-level, OOP API.
tf.layers/tf.losses/tf.metrics	Libraries for common model components.
TensorFlow	Lower-level APIs

The two fundamental components of TensorFlow are:

1. A "graph protocol buffer"
2. A "runtime" that can execute the graph

The two-component mentioned above are similar to "Python" code and the "Python interpreter." Just as the "Python interpreter" can run Python code on several hardware systems, TensorFlow can be operated on various hardware systems, like CPU, GPU, and TPU.

To make a decision regarding which API(s) should be used, you must consider the API offering the highest abstraction level to solve the target problem. Easier to use, but (by design) less flexible, are the greater abstract levels. It is recommended to first begin with the highest-level API and make everything work. If for certain unique modeling issues, you need extra flexibility, move one level down. Notice that each level is constructed on the lower-level APIs. It should thus be quite simple to decrease the hierarchy.

For the development of the majority of Machine Learning models, we will use "tf.estimator" API, which significantly lowers the number of code lines needed for development. Also, "tf.estimator" is compatible with Scikit-Learn API.

Chapter 2:Machine Learning Algorithms

By utilizing prior computations and underlying algorithms, machines are now capable of learning from and training on their own to generate high-quality, readily reproducible decisions and results. The notion of machine learning has been around for a long time now, but the latest advances in machine learning algorithms have made extensive data processing and analysis feasible for computers. This is achieved by applying sophisticated and complicated mathematical calculations using high speed and frequency automation. Today's advanced computing machines are able to analyze humongous information quantities quickly and deliver quicker and more precise outcomes. Companies using machine learning algorithms have increased flexibility to change the training data set to satisfy their company needs and train the machines accordingly. These tailored algorithms of machine learning enable companies to define potential hazards and possibilities for development. Typically, machine learning algorithms are used in cooperation with artificial intelligence technology and cognitive techniques to create computers extremely efficient and extremely effective in processing large quantities of information or big data and generating extremely precise outcomes.

There are four fundamental types of machine learning algorithms available today:

Supervised Machine Learning Algorithms

Due to their ability to evaluate and apply the lessons learned from prior iterations and interactions to fresh input data set, the supervised learning algorithms are commonly used in predictive big data analysis. Based on the instructions given to predict and forecast future occurrences effectively, these algorithms can label all their ongoing runs. For instance, people can program the machine as "R" (Run), "N" (Negative) or "P" (Positive) to label its data points. The algorithm for machine learning will then label the input data as programmed and obtain data inputs with the right outputs. The algorithm will compare its own produced output to the "anticipated or correct" output, identifying future changes that can be created and fixing mistakes to make the model more precise and smarter. By using methods such as "regression," "prediction," "classification" and "ingredient boosting" to train the machine learning algorithms well, any new input data can be fed into the machine as a set of "target" data to orchestrate the learning program as desired. This "known training data set" jump-starts the analytical process followed by the learning algorithm to produce an "inferred feature" that can be used to generate forecasts and predictions based on output values for future occurrences. For instance, financial institutions and banks rely strongly on monitoring machine learning algorithms to detect credit card fraud and predict the probability of a prospective credit card client failing to make their credit payments on time.

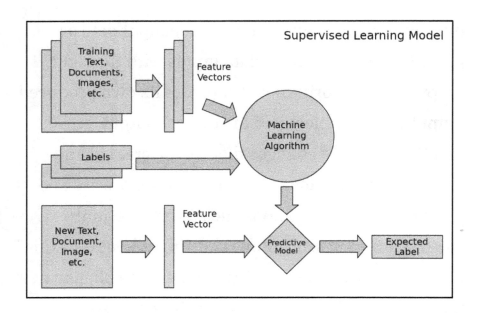

Unsupervised Machine Learning Algorithms

Companies often find themselves in a scenario where information sources are inaccessible that are needed to produce a labeled and classified training data set. Using unsupervised ML algorithms is perfect in these circumstances. Unsupervised ML algorithms are widely used to define how the machine can generate "inferred features" to elucidate a concealed construct from the stack of unlabeled and unclassified data collection. These algorithms can explore the data in order to define a structure within the data mass. Unlike the supervised machine learning algorithms, the unsupervised algorithms fail to identify the correct output, although they are just as effective as the supervised learning algorithms in investigating input data and drawing inferences. These algorithms can be used to identify information outliers, generate tailored and custom product recommendations, classify text subjects using methods such as "self-organizing maps," "singular value decomposition" and "k-means clustering." For instance, customer identification with shared shopping characteristics that can be segmented into particular groups and focused on comparable marketing strategies and campaigns. As a result, in the online marketing world, unsupervised learning algorithms are extremely popular.

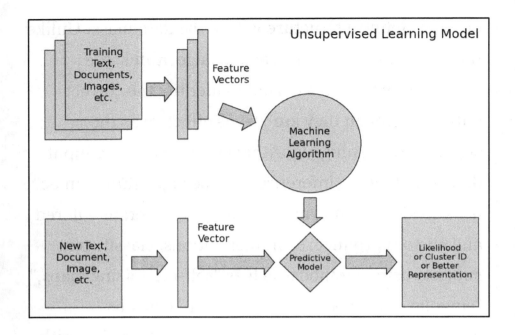

Semi-Supervised Machine Learning Algorithms

Highly versatile, the "semi-supervised machine learning algorithms" are capable of using both labeled and unlabeled information set to learn from and train themselves. These algorithms are a "hybrid" of algorithms that are supervised and unsupervised. Typically, with a small volume of labeled data, the training data set is comprised of predominantly unlabeled data. The use of analytical methods, including "forecast," "regression" and "classification" in conjunction with semi-supervised learning algorithms enable the machine to enhance its learning precision and training capabilities considerably. These algorithms are commonly used in instances where it is highly resource-intensive and less cost-effective for the business to generate labeled training data set from raw unlabeled data. Companies use semi-supervised learning algorithms on their systems to avoid incurring extra costs of staff and equipment. For instance, the implementation for "facial recognition" technology needs a huge amount of facial data distributed across various sources of input. The raw data pre-processing, processing, classification and labeling, acquired from sources such as internet cameras, needs a lot of resources and thousands of hours of job to be used as a training data set.

Reinforcement Machine Learning Algorithms

The "reinforcement machine learning algorithms" are much more distinctive in that they learn from the environment. These algorithms conduct activities and record the outcomes of each action diligently, which would have been either a failure resulting in mistake or reward for good performance. The two primary features that differentiate the reinforcement learning algorithms are the research method of "trial and error" and feedback loop of "delayed reward." Using a range of calculations, the computer constantly analyzes input data and sends a reinforcement signal for each right or anticipated output to ultimately optimize the end result. The algorithm develops a straightforward action and rewards feedback loop to evaluate, record, and learn which actions have been effective, and in a shorter period of time have resulted in correct or expected output. The use of these algorithms allows the system to automatically determine optimal behaviors and maximize its efficiency within the constraints of a particular context. The reinforcement machine learning algorithms are therefore strongly used in gaming, robotics engineering, and navigation systems.

The machine learning algorithms have proliferated to hundreds and thousands and counting. Here are some of the most widely used algorithms:

Regression

The "regression" techniques fall under the category of supervised machine learning. They help predict or describe a particular numerical value based on the set of prior information, such as anticipating the cost of a property based on previous cost information for similar characteristics. Regression techniques vary from simple (such as "linear regression") to complex (such as "regular linear regression", "polynomial regression", "decision trees", "random forest regression" and "neural networks", among others).

The simplest method of all is **"linear regression,"** where the line's "mathematical equation (y= m*x+b) is used to model the data collection". Multiple "data pairs (x, y)" can train a "linear regression" model by calculating the position and slope of a line that can decrease the total distance between the data points and the line. In other words, the calculation of the "slope (m)" and "y-intercept (b)" is used for a line that produces the highest approximation for data observations.

For example, using the "linear regression" technique to generate predictions for the energy consumption (in kWh) of houses by collecting the age of the house, no. of bedrooms, square footage area and a number of installed electronic equipment. Now, we have more than one input (year built, square footage) it is possible to use "linear multi-variable regression." The underlying process is the same as "one-to-one linear regression," however, the line created was based on the number of variables in multi-dimensional space.

The plot below demonstrates how well the model of linear regression fits real construction energy consumption. In case where you could gather house characteristics such as year built and square footage, but you don't understand the house's energy consumption then you are better off using the fitted line to generate approximations for the house's energy consumption.

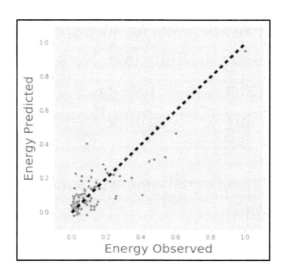

Multiple Linear Regression tends to be the most common form of "regression" technique used in data science and the majority of statistical tasks. Just like the "linear regression" technique, there will be an output variable "Y" in "multiple linear regression." However, the distinction now is that we're going to have numerous "X" or independent variables generating predictions for "Y".

For instance, a model developed for predicting the cost of housing in Washington DC will be driven by "multiple linear regression" technique. The cost of housing in Washington DC will be the "Y" or dependent variable for the model. "X" or the independent variables for this model will include data points such as vicinity to public transport, schooling district, square footage, number of rooms, which will eventually determine the market price of the housing.

The mathematical equation for this model can be written as below:

$$\text{``housing\_price} = \beta_0 + \beta_1\, sq\_foot + \beta_2\, dist\_transport + \beta_3\, num\_rooms\text{''}$$

Polynomial Regression – Our models developed a straight line in the last two types of "regression" techniques. This straight line is a result of the connection between "X" and "Y" which is "linear" and does not alter the influence "X" has on "Y" as the changing values of "X." Our model will lead in a row with a curve in "polynomial regression".

If we attempted to fit a graph with non-linear features using "linear regression", it would not yield the best fit line for the non-linear features. For instance, the graph on the left shown in the picture below has the scatter plot depicting an upward trend, but with a curve. A straight line does not operate in this situation. Instead, we will generate a line with a curve to match the curve in our data with a polynomial regression, like the chart on the right shown in the picture below. The equation of a polynomial will appear like the linear equation, the distinction being that one or more of the "X" variables will be linked to some polynomial expression. For instance,

$$"Y = mX^2 + b"$$

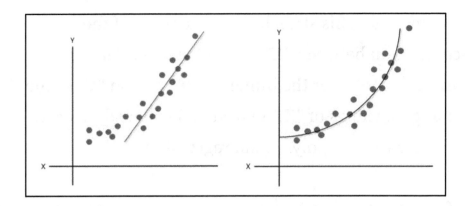

Another technique of reduction is called **"LASSO regression."** A very complementary technique to the "ridge regression," "lasso regression" promotes the use of simpler and leaner models to generate predictions. In lasso regression, the model reduces the value of coefficients relatively more rigidly. LASSO stands for the "least absolute shrinkage and selection operator." Data on our scatterplot, like the mean or median values of the data are reduced to a more compact level. We use this when the model is experiencing high multicollinearity similar to the "ridge regression" model.

A hybrid of "LASSO" and "ridge regression" methods is known as **"ElasticNet Regression."** Its primary objective is to enhance further the accuracy of the predictions generated by the "LASSO regression" technique. "ElasticNet Regression" is a confluence of both "LASSO" and "ridge regression" techniques of rewarding smaller coefficient values. All three of these designs are available in the R and Python "Glmnet suite."

"Bayesian regression" models are useful when there is a lack of sufficient data, or available data has poor distribution. These regression models are developed based on probability distributions rather than data points, meaning the resulting chart will appear as a bell curve depicting the variance with the most frequently occurring values in the center of the curve. The dependent variable "Y" in "Bayesian regression" is not valuation but a probability. Instead of predicting a value, we try to estimate the probability of an occurrence. This is regarded as "frequentist statistics," and this sort of statistics is built on the "Bayes theorem."

"Frequentist statistics" hypothesize if an event is going to occur and the probability of it happening again in the future.

"Conditional probability" is integral to the concept of "frequentist statistics." Conditional probability pertains to the events whose results are dependent on one another. Events can also be conditional, which means the preceding event can potentially alter the probability of the next event. Assume you have a box of M&Ms and you want to understand the probability of withdrawing distinct colors of the M&Ms from the bag. If you have a set of three yellow M&Ms and three blue M&Ms and on your first draw, you get a blue M&M. With your next draw from the box, the probability of taking out a blue M&M will be lower than the first draw. This is a classic example of "conditional probability." On the other hand, an independent event is flipping of a coin, meaning the preceding coin flip doesn't alter the probability of the next flip of the coin.

Therefore, a coin flip is not an example of "conditional probability."

Classification

The method of "classification" is another class of "supervised machine learning," which can generate predictions or explanations for a "class value." For example, this method can be used to predict if an online customer will actually purchase a particular product. The result generated will be reported as a yes or no response, i.e., "buyer" or "not a buyer." But techniques of classification are not restricted to two classes. A classification technique, for instance, could assist in evaluating whether a specified picture includes a sedan or an SUV. The output will be three different values in this case: 1) the picture contains a sedan, 2) the picture contains an SUV, or 3) the picture does not contain either a sedan or an SUV.

"Logistic regression" is considered the easiest classification algorithm, though the term comes across as a "regression" technique that is far from reality. "Logistic regression" generates estimations for the likelihood of an event taking place based on single or multiple input values. For example, to generate estimation for the likelihood of a student being accepted to a specific university, a "logistic regression" will use the standardized testing scores and university testing scores for a student as inputs. The generated prediction is a probability, ranging between '0' and '1', where 1 is full assurance. For the student, if the estimated likelihood is more significant than 0.5, then the prediction would be that they will be accepted. If the projected probability is less than 0.5, the prediction would be that they will be denied admission.

The following graph shows the ratings of past learners as well as whether they have been accepted. Logistic regression enables the creation of a line that can represent the "decision boundary."

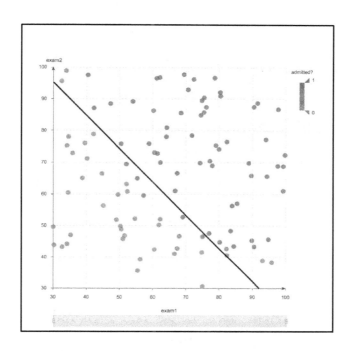

Clustering

We enter the category of unsupervised machine learning, with "clustering methods" because its objective is to "group or cluster observations with comparable features." Clustering methods do not use output data to train but allow the output to be defined by the algorithm. Only data visualizations can be used in clustering techniques to check the solution's quality.

"K-Means clustering," where 'K' is used to represent the number of "clusters" that the customer elects to generate and is the most common clustering method. (Note that different methods for selecting K value, such as the "elbow technique," are available.)

Steps used by K-Means clustering to process the data points:

1. The data centers are selected randomly by 'K.'
2. Assigns each data point to the nearest centers that have been randomly generated.
3. Re-calculates each cluster's center.
4. If centers do not change (or have minor change), the process will be completed. Otherwise, we'll go back to step 2. (Set a maximum amount of iterations in advance to avoid getting stuck in an infinite loop, if the center of the cluster continues to alter.)

The following plot applies "K-Means" to a building data set. Each column in the plot shows each building's efficiency. The four measurements relate to air conditioning, heating, installed electronic appliances (refrigerators, TV), and cooking gas. For simplicity of interpretation of the results, 'K' can be set to value '2' for clustering, wherein one cluster will be selected as an efficient building group and the other cluster as an inefficient building group. You see the place of the structures on the left as well as a couple of the building characteristics used as inputs on the right: installed electronic appliances and heating.

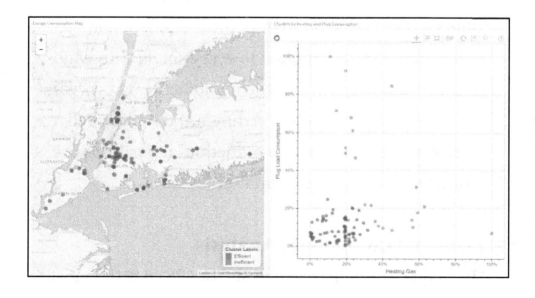

Dimension Reduction

As the name indicates, to extract the least significant information (sometimes redundant columns) from a data set, we use "dimensionality reduction". In practice, date sets tend to contain hundreds or even thousands of rows (also known as characteristics), which makes it essential to reduce the total number of rows. For example, pictures may contain thousands of pixels, all those pixels are not important for the analysis. Or a large number of measurements or experiments can be applied to every single chip while testing microchips within the manufacturing process, majority of which produce redundant data. In such scenarios, "dimensionality reduction" algorithms are leveraged to manage the data set.

Principal Component Analysis

"Principal Component Analysis" or (PCA) is the most common "dimension reduction technique", which decreases the size of the "feature space" by discovering new vectors that are capable of maximizing the linear variety of the data. When the linear correlations of the data are powerful, PCA can dramatically decrease the data dimension without losing too much information. PCA is one of the fundamental algorithms of machine learning. It enables you to decrease the data dimension, losing as little information as possible. It is used in many fields such as object recognition, vision of computers, compression of information, etc. The calculation of the main parts is limited to the calculation of the initial data's own vectors and covariance matrix values or to the data matrix's unique decomposition. Through one we can convey several indications, merge, so to speak, and operate with a simpler model already. Of course, most probably, data loss will not be avoided, but the PCA technique will assist us to minimize any losses.

t-Stochastic Neighbor Embedding (t-SNE)
Another common technique is "t-Stochastic Neighbor Embedding (t-SNE)", which results in decrease of non-

linear dimensionality. This technique is primarily used for data visualization, with potential use for machine learning functions such as space reduction and clustering.

The next plot demonstrates "MNIST database" analysis of handwritten digits. "MNIST" includes a large number of digit pictures from 0 to 9, used by scientists to test "clustering" and "classification" algorithms. Individual row of the data set represents "vectorized version" of the original picture (size 28x28 = 784 pixels) and a label (0, 1, 2 and so on) for each picture. Note that the dimensionality is therefore reduced from 784 pixels to 2-D in the plot below. Two-dimensional projecting enables visualization of the initial high-dimensional data set.

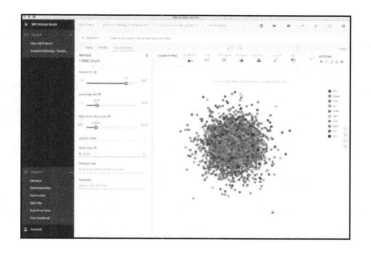

Ensemble Methods

Think that you have chosen to construct a car because you are not pleased with the variety of cars available in the market and online. You may start by discovering the best option for every component that you need. The resulting car will outshine all the other alternatives with the assembly of all these excellent components.

"Ensemble methods" use the same concept of mixing several predictive models (controlled machine learning) to obtain results of greater quality than any of the models can generate on their own. The "Random Forest" algorithms, for instance, is an "ensemble method" that collates various trained "Decision Trees" with different data set samples. Consequently, the quality of predictions generated by "Random Forest" method is better than the quality of the estimated predictions generated by only one "Decision Tree". Think of "ensemble methods" as an approach for reducing a single machine learning model's variance and bias. This is essential because under certain circumstances, any specified model may be accurate but completely incorrect under other circumstances. The relative accuracy could be overturned with another model. The quality of the predictions is balanced by merging the two models.

Transfer Learning

Imagine you are a data scientist focusing on the clothing industry. You have been training a high-quality learning model for months to be able to classify pictures of "women's tops" as tops, tank tops, and blouses. You have been tasked to create a comparable model for classification of pants pictures such as jeans, trousers, and chinos. With the use of the "Transfer Learning" method, the understanding incorporated into the first model be seamlessly transferred and applied to the second model.

Transfer Learning pertains to the re-use and adaptation of a portion of a previously trained neural network to a fresh but comparable assignment. Specifically, once a neural network has been successfully trained for a particular task, a proportion of the trained layers can be easily transferred and combined with new layers that are then trained on pertinent data for the new task. This new "neural network" can learn and adapt rapidly to the new assignment by incorporating a few layers.

The primary benefit of transferring learning is decreased in the volume of data required to train the neural network resulting in cost savings for the development of "deep learning algorithms." Not to forget how hard it can be even to procure a sufficient amount of labeled data to train the model.

Suppose, in this example, you are using a neural network with 20 hidden layers for the "women's top" model. You understand after running a few tests that 16 of the women's top model layers can be transferred and combined them with a new set of data to train on pants pictures. Therefore, the new pants model will have 17 concealed layers. The input and output of both the tasks are distinct, but the reusable layers are capable of summarizing the data appropriate to both, e.g., clothing, zippers, and shape of the garment.

Transfer learning is getting increasingly popular, so much so that for basic "deep learning tasks" such as picture and text classification, a variety of high quality pre-trained models are already available in the market.

Natural Language Processing

A majority of the knowledge and information pertaining to our world is in some type of human language. Once deemed as impossible to achieve, today, computers are capable of reading large volumes of books and blogs within minutes. Although computers are still unable to comprehend "human text fully", but they can be trained to perform specific tasks. Mobile devices, for instance, can be trained to auto-complete text messages or fix spelling mistakes. Machines have been trained enough to hold straightforward conversations like humans.

"Natural Language Processing" (NLP) is not exactly a method of ML; instead, it is a commonly used technique to produce texts for machine learning. Consider a multitude of formats of tons of text files (words, internet blogs, etc.) Most of these text files are usually flooded with typing errors, grammatically incorrect characters and phrases that need to be filtered out. The most popular text processing model available in the market today is "NLTK (Natural Language ToolKit)," developed by "Stanford University" researchers.

The easiest approach to map texts into numerical representations is the calculation of the frequency of each word contained in every text document. For example, an integer matrix where individual rows represent one text document and every column represents a single word. This word frequency representation matrix is frequently referred to as the "Term Frequency Matrix" (TFM). From there, individual matrix entries can be separated by weight of how essential every single term is within the whole stack of papers. This form of the matrix representation of a text document is called "Term Frequency Inverse Document Frequency" (TFIDF), which usually yields better performance for machine learning tasks.

Word Embedding

"Term Frequency Matrix" and "Term Frequency Inverse Document Frequency" are numerical representations of text papers that only take into account frequency and weighted frequencies to represent text files. On the other hand, "Word

Embedding" in a document is capable of capturing the actual context of a word. Embedding can quantify the similarity between phrases within the context of the word, which subsequently allows the execution of arithmetic operations with words.

"Word2Vec" is a neural network-based technique that can map phrases to a numerical vector in a corpus. These vectors are then used to discover synonyms, do arithmetic with words or phrases, or to represent text files. Let's suppose, for instance, a large enough body of text files was used to estimate word embedding. Suppose the words "king, queen, man, and female" are found in the corpus and vector ("word") is the number vector representing the word "word." We can conduct an arithmetic procedure with numbers to estimate vector('woman'):

$vector('king') + vector('woman') - vector('man') \sim vector('queen')$

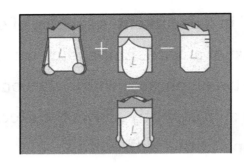

Word depictions enable similarities to be found between phrases by calculating the "cosine similarity" between the vector representation of the two words. The "cosine similarity" gives a measure of the angle between two vectors.

We use machine learning techniques to calculate word embedding, but this is often a preliminary step in implementing a machine learning algorithm on top of the word embedding method. For example, the "Twitter" user database containing a large volume of "tweets" can be leveraged to understand which of these customers purchased a house recently. We can merge "Word2Vec" with logistic regression to generate predictions on the likelihood of a new "Twitter" user purchasing a home.

Decision Trees

To refresh your memory; a machine learning decision tree can be defined as "a tree-like graphical representation of the decision-making process, by taking into consideration all the conditions or factors that can influence the decision and the consequences of those decisions." Decision trees are considered one of the simplest "supervised machine learning algorithms," with three main elements: "branch nodes" representing conditions of the data set, "edges" representing the ongoing decision process and "leaf nodes" representing the end of the decision.

The two types of decision trees are: "Classification tree" that is used to classify Data on the basis of the existing data available in the system; "Regression tree" which is used to make a forecast for predictions for future events on the basis of the existing data in the system. Both of these trees are heavily used in machine learning algorithms. A widely used terminology for decision trees is "Classification and Regression trees" or "CART."

Let's look at how you can build a simple decision tree based on a real-life example.

Step 1: Identify what decision needs to be made, which will serve as a "root node" for the decision tree. For this example, a decision needs to be made on "What would you like to do over the weekend?". Unlike real trees, the decision tree has its roots on top instead of the bottom.

Step 2: Identify conditions or influencing factors for your decision which will serve as "branch nodes" for the decision tree. For this example, conditions could include "would you like to spend the weekend alone or with your friends?" and "how is the weather going to be?".

Step 3: As you answer the conditional questions, you may run into additional conditions that you might have ignored. You will now continue to your final decision by processing all the conditional questions individually. These bifurcations will serve as "edges" of your decision tree.

Step 4: Once you have processed all of the permutations and combinations and eventually made your final decision, that final decision will serve as the "leaf node" of your decision tree. Unlike "branch nodes," there are no further bifurcations possible from a "leaf node."

Here is the graphical representation of your decision for the example above:

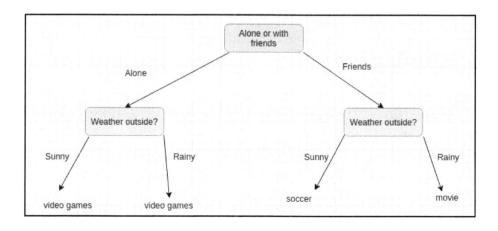

As you would expect from a decision tree, you have obtained a "model representing a set of sequential and hierarchical decisions that ultimately lead to some final decision." This example is at a very high-level to help you develop an understanding of the concept of decision trees. The data science and machine learning decision trees are much more complicated and bigger with hundreds and thousands of branch nodes and edges.

The best tool on the market to visualize and understand decision trees is "Scikit Learn." Machine learning decisions tree models can be developed using two steps: "Induction" and "Pruning."

Induction

In this step, the decision trees are actually developed by selecting and modeling all of the sequential and hierarchical decision boundaries on the basis of the existing data set. For your ease of understanding, here are four high-level steps required to develop the tree:

1. Gather, classify, and label the training data set with "feature variables" and "classification or regression output."

2. Identify the best and most cost-effective feature within the training data set that will be used as the point for bifurcating the data.

3. Based on the possible values of the selected "best feature," create subsets of data by bifurcating the data set. These bifurcations will define the "branch nodes" of the decision tree, wherein each node serves as a point of bifurcation based on specific features from the data set.

4. Iteratively develop new tree nodes with the use of data subsets gathered from Step 3. These bifurcations will continue until an optimal point is reached, where maximum accuracy is achieved while minimizing the number of bifurcations or nodes.

Pruning

The inherent purpose of decision trees is to support training and self-learning of the system, which often requires overloading of all possible conditions and influencing factors that might affect the final result. To overcome the challenge of setting the correct output for the least number of instances per node, developers make a "safe bet" by settling for that "least number" as rather small. This results in a high number of bifurcations on necessary, making for a very complex and large decision tree. This is where "tree pruning" comes into the picture. The verb "prune" literally means "to reduce, especially by eliminating the superfluous matter." This is the same kind of concept taken from real-life tree pruning and applied to the data science and machine learning decision tree pruning process.

The process of pruning effectively reduces the overall complexity of the decision tree by "transforming and compressing strict and rigid decision boundaries into generalized and smooth boundaries." The number of bifurcations in the decision trees determines the overall complexity of the tree. The easiest and widely used pruning method is reviewing individual branch nodes and evaluating the effect of its removal on the cost function of the decision tree. If the cost function has little to no effect of the removal, then the branch node under review can be easily removed or "pruned."

Apriori Machine Learning Algorithm

"Apriori algorithm" is another unsupervised ML algorithm that can produce rules of the association from a specified set of data. "Association rule" simply means if an item X exists, then item Y has a predefined probability of existence. Most rules of the association are produced in the format of "IF-THEN" statements. For instance, "IF" someone purchases an iPhone, "THEN" they have most likely purchased an iPhone case as well. The Apriori algorithm is able to draw these findings by initially observing the number of individuals who purchased an iPhone case while making an iPhone purchase and generating a ratio obtained by dividing the number individuals who bought a new iPhone (1000) with individuals who also bought an iPhone case (800) with their new iPhones.

The fundamental principles of Apriori ML Algorithm are:

- If a set of events have a high frequency of occurrence, then all subsets of that event set will also have a high frequency of occurrence.
- If a set of events occur occasionally, then all supersets of the event set of will sometimes occur as well.

Apriori algorithm has broad applicability in the following areas:

- **"Detecting Adverse Drug Reactions"**

"Apriori algorithm" is used to analyze healthcare data such as the drugs administered to the patient, characteristics of each patient, harmful side effects experienced by the patient, the original diagnosis, among others. This analysis generates rules of association that provide insight into the characteristics of the patient and the administered drug that potentially contributed to the adverse side effects of the drug.

- **"Market Basket Analysis"**

Some of the leading online e-commerce businesses including "Amazon," use the Apriori algorithm to gather insights on products that have a high likelihood of being bought together and products that can have an upsell with product promotions and discount offers. For instance, Apriori could be used by a retailer to generate predictions such as customers purchasing sugar and flour have a high likelihood of buying eggs to bake cookies and cakes.

- **"Auto-Complete Applications"**

The highly cherished auto-complete feature on "Google" is another common Apriori application. When the user starts typing in their keywords for a search, the search engine searches its database, for other related phrases that are usually typed in after a particular word.

Support vector machine learning algorithm

"Support Vector Machine" or (SVM) is a type of "supervised ML algorithm," used for "classification" or "regression," where the data set trains SVM on "classes" in order to be able to classify new inputs. This algorithm operates by classifying the data into various "classes" by discovering a line (hyperplane) that divides the collection of training data into "classes." Due to the availability of various linear hyper-planes, this algorithm attempts to maximize the distance between the different "classes" involved, which is called as "margin maximization." By identifying the line that maximizes the class distance, the likelihood of generalizing apparent to unseen data can be improved.

SVM's can be categorized into two as follows:

- "Linear SVM's" – The training data or classifiers can be divided by a hyper-plane.
- "Non-Linear SVM's" – Unlike linear SVMs, in "non-linear SVM's" the possibility to separate the training data with a hyper-plane is nonexistent. For example, the Face Detection training data consists of a group of facial images and another group of non-facial images. The training data is so complicated under such circumstances that it is difficult to obtain a feature representation of every single vector. It is extremely complex to separate the facial data set linearly from the non-facial data set.

Different economic organizations widely use SVM for stock market forecasting. For example, SVM is leveraged to compare relative stock performances of various stocks in the same industrial sector. The classifications generated by SVM, aids in the investment-related decision-making process.

The Kernel Trick

The data collected in the real world is randomly distributed and making it too difficult to separate different classes linearly. However, if we can potentially figure out a way to map the data from 2-dimensional space to 3-dimensional space, as shown in the picture below, we will be able to discover a decision surface that obviously separates distinct classes.

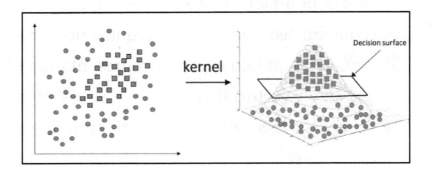

One approach to transform data like this is mapping all data points to a higher dimension (in this case, three dimensions), finding the limit, and making the classification. That works for a limited number of dimensions, but computations within a given space become increasingly costly when there are a lot of dimensions to deal with. And so the kernel trick comes to the rescue!

The "kernel trick" enables us to function in the original feature space without needing to calculate the data coordinates in a higher-dimensional space. For example, the equation in the picture below has a couple of 3-D data points as 'x' and 'y.'

$$\mathbf{x} = (x_1, x_2, x_3)^T$$
$$\mathbf{y} = (y_1, y_2, y_3)^T$$

Suppose we want to map 'x' and 'y' to nine-dimensional space. To get the final outcome, which would be just scalar, we have to do the calculations shown in the picture below. In this case, the computational complexity will be O(n2).

$$\phi(\mathbf{x}) = (x_1^2, x_1x_2, x_1x_3, x_2x_1, x_2^2, x_2x_3, x_3x_1, x_3x_2, x_3^2)^T$$
$$\phi(\mathbf{y}) = (y_1^2, y_1y_2, y_1y_3, y_2y_1, y_2^2, y_2y_3, y_3y_1, y_3y_2, y_3^2)^T$$

$$\phi(\mathbf{x})^T\phi(\mathbf{y}) = \sum_{i,j=1}^{3} x_i x_j y_i y_j$$

However, by using the "kernel function," which is denoted as 'k (x, y)', instead of doing the complex calculations in the 9-dimensional space, the same outcome can be achieved in the 3-dimensional space by calculating the "dot product" of 'x-transpose' and 'y'. In this case, the computational complexity will be O(n).

$$k(\mathbf{x}, \mathbf{y}) = (\mathbf{x}^T\mathbf{y})^2$$
$$= (x_1y_1 + x_2y_2 + x_3y_3)^2$$
$$= \sum_{i,j=1}^{3} x_i x_j y_i y_j$$

In principle, the kernel trick is used to make the transformation of data into higher dimensions much more effectively and less costly. The use of the kernel trick is not restricted to the SVM algorithm. The kernel trick can be used with any computations involving the "dot products (x, y)".

Chapter 3: Fundamentals and Importance of Artificial Intelligence

Ever wondered what is "intelligence" and how some of us are considered to be more intelligent than others? How do we claim that certain people are wired differently from the rest of us "commoners," and turn out to be the "Einsteins" and "Newtons" of the world? It goes without saying that human beings are residing at the pinnacle of the biological pyramid as the superior most species to have ever been created through the course of evolution. But even the highly sophisticated and complex behavioral activities displayed by animals are never ascribed as intelligent. We fail to acknowledge the marvelous coordination and discipline of the ant colonies or the impeccable order of hierarchy and self-organization exhibited by a swarm of bees. Some of the researchers embarked on this journey to discover how intelligent the animals can really be, so they conducted an experiment on female digger wasps. The researchers manipulated with the location of the food gathered by the wasps before depositing it in the burrow. The wasps inherently verify the burrow for intruders and leave the food near the entrance before depositing it inside. But with the food being displaced a few inches off of the entrance, the wasps would fail to adapt to the changing circumstances and thereby, fail to deposit the food inside the burrow. This idea is crucial to stop assuring the fact learning and changing are integral to "intelligence."

Psychology experts have categorized "human intelligence" as a fine blend of a variety of mental abilities including the ability to learn from life experiences, ability to adapt to changing environments, ability to understand abstract concepts, logical reasoning, perception, ability to use language and problem-solving abilities. Human beings have not only been experimenting on animals to detect signs of intelligence for the greater good, but we have also been experimenting with machines to impart them human-like intelligence. And this is where the concept of "Artificial Intelligence" was born.

In the mid 20th Century, the pioneering British Computer Scientist, Alan Turing, had laid the foundation of artificial intelligence technology, with the development of an abstract machine with a scanner and limitless memory, that was capable of altering and improving its own programming implying a learning capability. Today, this machine serves as a basis for development and enhancement to the modern computer and is famously known as "Turing machine." Eventually, in 1956, the term artificial intelligence or AI was coined and can be defined as the science of developing machines and computers, that are controlled and operated by human beings, but capable of mirroring and manifesting human intelligence to achieve a set goal. Unlike the picture painted in our minds by the entertainment industry, artificial intelligence is much more than robots coming to life to take vengeance on and overpower humanity. The artificial intelligence-based machines and computers are being developed with superficial abilities to think and act like humans. They are literally being wired to be able to rationalize ideas and duplicate actions that are generally taken by humans to fulfill a targeted goal.

The ability to learn, reason, and perceive are considered as the three fundamental goals of Artificial Intelligence. Some of the core human mental abilities that researchers are aspiring to mimic in computers and machines are:

1. **Knowledge** –A large volume of data is required by the machines to be able to understand and process the world as it is. Seamless access to data objects, categories, properties, and relationships that are stored and managed using data storage is critical to developing knowledge engineering for artificial.

2. **Learning** – the Evergreen trial and error method tends to be the simplest form of learning applicable to artificial intelligence technology. You will be learning about machine learning in-depth in the chapter titled "Machine Learning and Artificial Intelligence.".

3. **Problem Solving** – "The systematic process to reach a predefined goal or solution by searching through a range of possible actions" can be defined as problem-solving. A general-purpose problem-solving method can be used to resolve different kinds of problems and is frequently used in artificial intelligence.

4. **Reasoning** – The ability to draw inferences in accordance with the situation at hand is referred to as the act of reasoning. Two widely known forms of reasoning are "deductive reasoning" (assumes the conclusion is true if the premise is true) and "inductive reasoning" (the conclusion could or could not be true, even if the premise is true). Implementation of "true reasoning" is one of the most difficult challenges in the development and advancement of artificial intelligence technology.

5. **Perception** – perception pertains to the process of generating a 3-D view of an object with the use of various sensory organs and is directly affected by the surrounding environment. Artificial

perception has already given rise to self-driving cars and incapable of collecting and delivering products.

Importance of Artificial Intelligence

To get a sense of how important Artificial Intelligence is in our daily lives, it would be easier to state what part of our modern lifestyle has not been touched by it. Every facet of human life is being influenced by the "intelligent machines" designed to augment human capabilities and enhance efficiencies. Artificial Intelligence is the central tenet of the Fourth Industrial Revolution that could potentially dispute our ideas about what it means to be "human."

Here are a few reasons to help you understand that Artificial Intelligence is important for your business right now:

- Automation of repetitive learning and discovery from data. Unlike hardware-driven robotic automation that tends to automate manual tasks, AI performs high frequency, high volume, computer-based tasks constantly and reliably. However, for AI automation, the human inquiry continues to be necessary to set up the system and ask pertinent questions.

- We are adding intelligence to already available products. The way Siri was added to the new generation of iPhones, AI would also be used to enhance the capabilities of products that we already use. It's impossible to sell AI as a self only application. Technologies at home and in the workplace, like investment analysis or network security, can be improved significantly by combining a large amount of data with automation, smart machines, robots, and conversational platforms.

- Progressive learning algorithms will help AI adapt to the changing world. Machine learning allows for the program to learn, take note, and improve upon its errors. To aid the algorithm is acquiring skills, AI finds structure and patterns in the data, making the algorithm function as a classifier or a predictor. Similar to how the algorithm has taught itself how to play chess, it can also teach itself what online products should be recommended next. The beauty of this model is that it adapts with every new set of data. If the first response is deemed incorrect, an AI technique called Backpropagation allows the model to adjust using the new available date and training.

- AI is making an analysis of a deeper and larger data set with the use of neural networks containing multiple hidden layers. Think about it—a fraud detection system with multiple hidden layers could only be built in a dream just a few years ago. With the advent of big data and never before imagined computer powers, a whole new world awaits us. Data to the machines is like the gas to your vehicles, the more data you can feed them, the results are faster and accurate. Deep learning models thrive on the excess of data because they learn directly from the data.

- Unbelievable accuracy has been achieved through the deep neural networks of the AI. For example, the more we use Alexa and Google Search, the more accurate they become because they are based on deep learning. These deep neural networks are also empowering our medical field. Image classification and object recognition are now capable of finding cancer on MRIs with similar accuracy as that of a highly trained radiologist.
- AI helps to bring out the best out of the data. Today data is its own currency, and when algorithms are self-learning, it can easily become intellectual property. The raw data is like a gold mine, the more and deeper you dig, the more gold that is the useful information you can dig out. Simply applying AI to the data can help you get to the right answers faster and makes for a competitive advantage. Remember the best data will always win, even though everybody is using similar techniques.

- Rapid implementation of AI technologies is allowing for new technologies to be introduced at an incredibly fast pace and can be challenging to keep up with. It's becoming increasingly important for more people to truly understand all of the implications AI can have on our world.
- The impact of AI on our society cannot be underestimated. As we expand the reach and application of AI in the world around us, it is sure to improve, transform, or create things that we can still not imagine.
- Technology giants like "Google" and "Amazon," are heavily investing in AI research and development, which goes to show the importance AI holds for businesses in general and by extension, the whole economy.
- AI will lead to legal implications across the globe, with nations requiring to review and update their laws and regulations in the light of AI policies. The use of AI in healthcare and transportation will require government scrutiny of the protected information being used by AI.

- Strong collaboration between Private and Public Sectors across the globe and not just the large tech companies is essential to successfully implement AI to serve humanity better. Our travel and hotel industries are already going through this revolution.

Industrial Application of Artificial Intelligence

Artificial Intelligence is leading the Fourth Industrial Revolution with its growing influence on everyday consumer products. AI has revamped the manufacturing, retail, and finance industries with new products, processes, and capabilities. Some of the most significant breakthroughs in physics and healthcare are also credited to AI. In this era of technological advancements as we move towards a future depicted in science fiction, AI has become an essential part of our world. Artificial Intelligence has exploded in recent years, thanks to the massive amount of online data we generate every day and the never seen before powerful computers. The business leaders and innovators are chasing the promise of AI to gain a competitive advantage while saving up on costs and time. From optimizing the delivery route to management of a global supply chain, AI is helping companies of all sizes across the industries to improve their bottom line with enhanced productivity. Companies are able to design, produce, and deliver superior products and services while cutting back on their expenses. Let's explore the application of Artificial Intelligence in all the major industries and how the business processes are changing to adopt AI.

Healthcare Industry

With the increasing availability of healthcare data, AI has brought on a paradigm shift to healthcare. The primary focus of Artificial Intelligence in the healthcare industry is the analysis of relationships between patient outcomes and the treatment or prevention technique used. AI programs have successfully been developed for patient diagnostics, treatment protocol generation, drug development, as well as patient monitoring and care. The powerful AI techniques can sift through a massive amount of clinical data and help unlock clinically relevant information to assist in decision making.

In 1965, Artificial Intelligence researcher "Edward Feigenbaum" and geneticist "Joshua Lederberg," developed the first major application of heuristic programming for chemical analysis called DENDRAL. This was the first-ever rule-based system that had real-world applications. Molecular structure illustration has been a substantive problem in organic chemistry since the chemical and physical properties of a compound are determined not just by the constituent atoms but by their geometric arrangement. Mass spectrometry could provide information about the constituent atoms but is insensitive to the geometry of the atoms. The ability of DENDRAL to hypothesize the molecular structure of a compound rivaled the performance of chemistry experts.

The DENDRAL laid the foundation of one of the most significant early uses of AI in medicine, in the form of an expert system called "MYCIN." In 1972, Stanford University began treating blood infections with the help of MYCIN. The patient's symptoms and medical test results were fed into "MYCIN" which could then suggest additional laboratory tests and request for further information regarding the patient to reach a probable diagnosis and even created recommendation for the treatment course. If desired, "MYCIN" could explain the reasoning behind its diagnosis. "MYCIN" was reported to have similar competence as that of the blood infection specialists and significantly better than general physicians. But due to its learning limitations, the "MYCIN" failed to gain popularity.

Some medical specialties with increasing AI research and use are:

- Radiology – The ability of AI to interpret imaging results supplements the clinician's ability to detect changes in an image that can easily be missed by the human eye. An AI algorithm recent created at Stanford University can detect specific sites in the lungs of the pneumonia patients.

- Electronic Health Records – The need for digital health records to optimize the information spread and access requires fast and accurate logging of all health-related data in the systems. A human is prone to errors and may be affected by cognitive overload and burnout. AI has successfully automated this process. The use of Predictive models on the electronic health records data allowed the prediction of individualized treatment response with 70-72% accuracy at baseline.

- Imaging – Ongoing AI research is helping doctors in evaluating the outcome of corrective jaw surgery as well as in assessing the cleft palate therapy to predict facial attractiveness.

Here are some of the most potent Artificial Intelligence advancements in healthcare:

- AI-assisted robotic surgery – The biggest draw of robot-assisted surgery is that they do not require large incisions and are considered minimally invasive with low post-op recovery time. Robots are capable of analyzing data from pre-op patient medical records and subsequently guiding the surgeon's instruments during surgery. These robot-assisted surgeries have reported up to a 21% reduction in patients' hospital stays. Robots can also use data from past surgeries and use AI to inform the surgeon about any new possible techniques. The most advanced surgical robot, "Da Vinci," allows surgeons to carry out complex surgical procedures with higher accuracy and greater control than the conventional methods.

- Supplement clinical diagnosis – Although the use of AI in diagnostics is still under the radar, a lot of successful use cases have already been reported. An algorithm created at Stanford University is capable of detecting skin cancer with similar competencies as that of a skilled dermatologist. An AI software program in Denmark was used to eavesdrop on emergency phone calls made to human dispatchers. The underlying algorithm analyzed the tone and words of the caller as well as the background noise to detect cases of a heart attack. The AI program had a 93% success rate which was 20% higher than the human counterparts.

- Virtual Nursing Assistants – The virtual nurses are available 24*7 without fatigue and lapse in judgment. They provide constant patient monitoring and directions for the most effective care while answering all of the patient's questions quickly and efficiently. An increase in regular communication between patients and their care providers can be credited to virtual nursing applications. This prevents unnecessary hospital visits and readmission. The virtual nurse assistant at Care Angel can already provide wellness checks through Artificial Intelligence and voice.

- Automation of administrative tasks – AI-driven technology such as voice to text transcriptions is aiding in ordering a test, prescribing medications, and even writing medical chart notes. The partnership between IBM and Cleveland Clinic has allowed IBM's Watson to perform mining on clinical health data and help physicians in developing personalized and more efficient treatment plans.

Finance or BankingIndustry

The tech giants tend to hog most of the limelight when it comes to cutting edge technological advancements. But the financial sector, including the stodgy banking incumbents, are showing increasing interest and signs of adoption of Artificial Intelligence. The banking or finance industry has a profound impact on virtually all consumers and businesses with a direct effect on the country's economy, so seeking insight and keeping up to date with the convergence of financial technology and Artificial Intelligence is critical for every business. The banking industry is putting its money on the Artificial Intelligence based solutions to address a lot of traditional banking problems such as providing quality customer service to their millions of customers, fraud prevention, mobile technology, and data security among others. Here are some popular Artificial Intelligence-based trends in banking.

Automation and Personalization of Customer Service with Chatbots

With the advancements in the natural language processing technology, the consumers' ability to distinguish between the human voice and the voice of a robot is increasingly diminishing. Chatbots with their more human-like voices and ability to resolve customer issues independently and in the absence of humanitarian assistance are the future of customer service, and it's bound to expand from banking to all other industries. The banks will soon be reporting huge savings and significant cost reductions in the next ten years. A recent study predicted up to $450 billion in savings by the banking and lending industry by 2030.

Despite this huge promise and reward brought on by AI-powered Chatbots, banking and other industries need to tread with caution when it comes to delivering service that meets or succeeds customer expectations. The reality is humans today and for the foreseeable future like to speak with another person to address and resolve their issues. The nuances of human problems seem too far-fetched to be understood by a callus robot. The best approach seems to be human customer service representatives augmented by the Chatbots rather than replacing humans completely. For example, the renowned Swiss bank UBS, with a global ranking of 35 for the volume of its assets, has partnered with Amazon. Amazon has successfully incorporated an "Ask UBS" service on its AI-powered speakers called Amazon Echo (Alexa). UBS customers across the world can simply "ask" Alexa for advice and analysis on global financial markets in lieu of The Wall Street Journal. The "Ask UBS" service is also designed to offer definitions and examples for the finance related jargon and acronyms. However, the "Ask UBS" application is unable to offer personalized advice to the UBS clients, owing to a lack of access to individual portfolios and client's holding and goals. This inability stems from security and privacy concerns regarding client data.

With the wealth of customer data including records of online and offline transactions and detailed demographics, the banking industry is sitting on a gold mine that needs the power of AI-based analytics to dig out the gold with data mining. Integration and analysis of information sourced from discrete databases have uniquely positioned banks to utilize Machine learning and obtain a complete view of their customers' needs and provide superior personalized services.

"The next step within the digital service model is for banks to price for the individual, and to negotiate that price in real-time, taking personalization to the ultimate level."
– James Eardley, SAP Marketing Director

For all the financial institutions, customer personalization has transcended from marketing and product customization into the realm of cybersecurity. Biometric data, like fingerprints, are increasingly being used to augment or replace traditional passwords and other means of identity verification. A recent study by "Google Intelligence," reported that by 2021, about 2 billion bank customers would be using some or other form of biometric identification. One of the leading tech giants, Apple, has descended onto payment platform and is now using their Artificial Intelligence-powered "facial recognition technology" to unlock their devices and also to validate payments, using their "digital wallet" service called "Apple Pay."

Fraud Prevention

The inherent capability of Artificial Intelligence to swiftly analyze large volumes of data and identify patterns that may not come naturally to the human observer has made AI the smoking gun for fraud detection and prevention. According to a recent report by McAfee global economy suffered a $600 billion loss through cybercrime alone. Real-time fraud detection is the only direct path to prevent fraud from happening in the first place. AI and machine learning-based solutions are empowering financial service providers with real-time fraud detection as well as reducing the frequency of legitimate transactions being flagged as fraudulent. The MasterCard company has reported an 80% decline in legitimate activity being marked as "false fraud," with its use of Artificial Intelligence technology.

Lending Risk Management

Banks and other money lending institutions bear high risk while giving out loans to the borrowers. This complex process of underwriting requires accuracy and high confidentiality. This is where AI swoops in to save the day, by analyzing available transaction data, market trends and recent financial activities pertinent to the prospective borrower and assessing potential risks in approving the loan(s).

Hedge Fund Management

Today, over $3 trillion in assets of the world economy are managed by hedge funds. The investment partnerships between investors or "limited partners" and professional fund managers are called hedge funds. Hedge fund's strategy to minimize the risk and maximize returns for the investors dictates the contribution made by the "limited partner" and the management of those funds by the general partner. The hedge funds epitomize the idiom "bigger the risk, bigger the reward" and are considered riskier investments. The hedge fund managers are responsible for shorting their stocks if they anticipate the market will drop or "hedge" by going long when they anticipate the market will grow. This stock trading can soon be taken over Artificial Intelligence based solutions requiring no human intervention and revolutionize the hedge fund management.

The ability of Artificial Intelligence powered machines to analyze massive amounts of data in a fraction of time then it takes a human and gather insight from its analysis to self-learn and improve its trading acumen is indeed a big winner. As intriguing as the use of AI to trade stocks appears, it is still missing the proof of concept, but nevertheless, companies are continuing to research and develop AI-powered systems that could potentially kick start a new era on Wall Street.

Here's how the top 7 commercial banks in America measure upon their use of Artificial Intelligence:

JP Morgan Chase

JP Morgan Chase has invested heavily in cutting edge technology with over $3 billion in 2016 alone. They recently introduced an AI-powered platform to review and analyze legal documents and extract essential client data called "Contact Intelligence" (COiN). COiN is capable of reviewing 12,000 annual commercial credit agreements in seconds. The same annual review takes over 360,000 human labor hours.

In 2015, for identification of customers with high receptiveness to subsequent equity offerings, Morgan Chase introduced the "Emerging Opportunities Engine" that can perform automated analysis on client data in the Equity Capital Markets. This AI-based solution is expected to be expanded for in their "Debt Capital Markets" among other areas.

In 2016, Morgan Chase deployed its virtual assistant technology that uses a "Natural Language Processing" interface to resolve employee's software-related service requests or tickets.

Wells Fargo

In February 2019, "Wells Fargo" announced the formation of a new team focused primarily on Artificial Intelligence Enterprise Solutions to leverage the AI technology for enhancement of their organizational structure. The AI solutions team is led by the Payments, Virtual Solutions, and Innovation group, which is focused on increasing connectivity for the company's payment efforts and advanced application programming interfaces to corporate customers.

Since 2009, Wells Fargo has leveraged the Facebook platform to communicate with its customers. In April 2019 the company rolled out an Artificial Intelligence-driven Chatbot through the Facebook Messenger application, for hundreds of their employees, in pilot mode. This Chatbot is capable of providing virtual assistance to its users by helping them reset their passwords and with pertinent account information.

Bank of America

Bank of America is dominating the Chatbot service in the banking industry since the launch of their Artificial Intelligence-powered virtual assistant called "Erica," which leverages cognitive messaging and predictive analysis, to provide financial guidelines to over 45 million Bank of America customers.

Bank of America's investment in technology can be easily observed with its mobile banking app that was launched a decade ago and now serves 22 million customers. Erica is designed as an integral component of the Bank of America mobile app and is available 24/7 to the customers. In addition, to be able to perform day to day transactions, Erica can anticipate unique financial needs to each client and provide 'smart recommendations' to help them achieve their financial goals.

"We want to be there for customers in the moments that matter most. Incorporating artificial intelligence into our mobile banking offering will help customers manage their simple banking needs more efficiently and consistently, which then allows our specialists in our financial centers to spend more time with customers to understand their more complex needs and help them improve their financial lives."
- Thong Nguyen, Bank of America

Citibank

Citibank has recently partnered with cutting edge technology companies through their investment and acquisitions wing, "Citi Ventures," to expand and improve its services. "Citi Ventures" has made a strategic investment in "Feedzai," which is a leading data science enterprise renowned for its real-time fraud identification and prevention techniques. Feedzai is able to identify questionable and/or fraudulent activities and conduct large scale analysis to alert the customer in a timely manner and prevent fraud.

Citi Ventures and RRE Ventures led the round two funding for an Artificial Intelligence-based platform called "Clarity Money." Citi Ventures is helping in the introduction of the Clarity Money app as the new personal financial app on the market, which can encourage customers to participate in third-party services aimed at improving overall financial health.

Transportation Industry

The transportation industry is highly susceptible to two problems arising from human errors, traffic, and accidents. These problems are too difficult to model owing to their inherently unpredictable nature but can be easily overcome with the use of Artificial Intelligence-powered tools that can analyze observed data and make or predict the appropriate decisions. The challenge of increasing travel demand, safety concerns, CO_2 emissions, and environmental degradation can be met with the power of artificial intelligence. From Artificial Neural Networks to Bee colony optimization, a whole lot of artificial intelligence techniques are being employed to make the transportation industry efficient and effective. To obtain significant relief from traffic congestion while making travel time more reliable for the population, transport authorities are experimenting with a variety of AI-based solutions. With the potential application of artificial intelligence for enhanced road infrastructure and assistance for drivers, the transportation industry it's focused on accomplishing a more reliable transport system, which will have limited to no effect on the environment while being cost-effective.

It is an uphill battle to fully understand the relationships between the characteristics of various transportation systems using traditional methods. Artificial intelligence is here once again to offer the panacea by transforming the traffic sensors on the road into a smart agent that can potentially detect accidents and predict future traffic conditions. Rapid development has been observed in the area of Intelligent Transport Systems (ITS), which are targeted to alleviate traffic congestion and improve the driving experience by utilizing multiple technologies and communication systems. They are capable of collecting and storing data that can be easily integrated with machine learning technology. To increase the efficiency of police patrol and keeping the citizens of safe collection of crime data is critical and can be achieved with the right AI-powered tools. Artificial intelligence can also simplify the transportation planning of the road freight transport system by providing accurate prediction methods to forecast its volume.

Here are some real-world examples of artificial intelligence being used in the transportation industry:

- Local motors company in collaboration with IBM's Watson has unveiled an AI-powered autonomous fully electric vehicle called "Olli."
- A highly promising traffic control system developed by Rapid Flow Technologies is called "SURTRAC," which allows traffic lights at intersections to respond to vehicular flow on an

individual level instead of being a part of a centralized system.

- A Chinese company called "TuSimple" entered the American market with their self-driving trucks that can utilize long-distance sensors with a complete observation range and it's deep learning artificial intelligence technology allows seamless detection and tracking of objects using multiple cameras.

- Rolls-Royce is expected to launch air own clueless cargo ships by 2020 that could be controlled remotely and pioneer the way for fully autonomous ships in the near future.

- In early 2019, the first autonomous trains were tested by the London underground train system that can potentially carry more passengers instead of driver's cabin.

- Some commuters in Sweden have reportedly been testing microchip implants on their bodies as travel tickets.

- China launched the Autonomous Rail Rapid Transit System (ART) in the city of Zhuzhou that doesn't require tracks and instead, the trains follow of virtual track created by painted dashed lines.

- Autonomous delivery trucks could soon be bringing our food and mail to us instead of the human-driven delivery service.

- Dubai is experimenting with Smart technology-driven digital number plates for cars, which can immediately send an alert to the authorities in the event of an accident.

- Some of the American airports are you using artificial intelligence as face-scanning technologies to verify the identities of passengers before allowing them to board the flight and ditching the traditional passports.

- The revolutionizing Google flight technology is able to predict flight delays before the airlines themselves by using advanced machine learning technology on the available data from previous flights and providing passengers a more accurate expected time of arrival.

- When it comes to real-time customer service, the Trainline app has surpassed all AI-powered applications on the market, with its BusyBot technology that can help the passengers with their change tickets booking and purchase as well as find a vacant seat on the train in real-time. This bot collects information from the passengers on board on how busy their carriages are and then analyzes that data to advise other passengers on potentially vacant seating.

- The "JOZU" app is aimed at once again liberating the modern woman who likes to travel alone and is concerned about her safety. It collects user data to provide women with the safest routes and methods of transport.

- China has pioneered the development of a smart highway that can charge electric vehicles as they are driving, and Australia is set to follow the lead. Smart roads are being designed to incorporate sensors to monitor traffic patterns and solar panels for vehicle charging.

- Smart luggage with built-in GPS tracker and weighing scales connected to your phones are already available on the market.

- Ford has recently announced its plan to file a patent for their Artificial Intelligence-based unmanned "Robotic Police Car" that can issue tickets for speeding and other violations to drivers by scanning their car registration and accessing the CCTV footage.

- Japan will soon be enjoying a new ride-hailing service. Sony recently announced the launch of its new service that will use Artificial Intelligence to manage fleets and provide an overview of potential traffic issues like congestions and detours due to public events.

- Ford has designed a "Smart City" with the system that allows smart vehicles to connect and coordinate with one another while cutting down on the risks of collisions and other accidents. The Smart city would collect data from its residents and share it with multiple smart technologies working in tandem to create a digital utopia.

Entertainment Industry

Artificial intelligence is increasingly running in the background of entertainment sources from video games to movies and serving us a richer, engaging, and more realistic experience. Entertainment providers such as Netflix and Hulu are using artificial intelligence to provide users personalized recommendations derived from individual user's historical activity and behavior. Computer graphics and digital media content producers have been leveraging Artificial Intelligence-based tools to enhance the pace and efficiency of their production processes. Movie companies are increasingly using machine learning algorithms in the development of film trailers and advertisements as well as pre-and post-production processes. For example, an artificial intelligence-powered tool called "RivetAI" allows producers to automate and excellent read the methods of movie script breakdown, storyboard as well as budgeting, scheduling, and generation of shot-list. Certain time-consuming tasks carried out during the post-production of the movies such as synchronization and assembly of the movie clips can be easily automated using artificial intelligence. Recently a team of AI researchers from The University of Illinois and The University of Washington successfully trained their artificial intelligence model to create new Flintstones video content, using an annotated video caption database that contained more than 25,000 Flintstones videos.

Marketing and Advertising

A machine learning algorithm can be easily trained with texts, stills, and video segments as data sources. It can then extract objects and concepts from these sources and recommend efficient marketing and advertising solutions. For example, an artificial intelligence-based tool called "Luban" was developed by Alibaba that can create banners at lightning speed in comparison to a human designer. In 2016, for the

Chinese online shopping extravaganza called "Singles Day, Luban generated a hundred and 17 million banner designs at a speed of 8000 banner designs per second.

The 20th Century Fox collaborated with IBM to use their AI system "Watson" for the creation of the trailer of their horror movie "Morgan." In order to learn the appropriate "moments" or clips that should appear in a standard horror movie trailer, Watson was trained to classify and analyze input "moments" from audio-visual and other composition elements from over a hundred horror movies. This training resulted in the creation of a six-minute movie trailer by Watson in a mere 24 hours, which would have taken a human professional weeks to produce.

With the use of Machine learning, computer vision technology, natural language processing, and predictive analytics, the marketing process can be accelerated exponentially through an AI marketing platform. For example, the artificial intelligence-based marketing platform developed by Albert Intelligence

Marketing is able to generate autonomous campaign management strategies, create customer solutions, and perform audience targeting. The company reported an 183% improvement in customer transaction rate and over 600% higher conversation efficiency, credited to the use of their AI-based platform.

In March 2016, artificial intelligence-based creative director called "AI-CD ß" was launched by McCann Erickson Japan as the first robotic creative director ever developed. "AI-CD ß" was given training on select elements of various TV shows and the winners from the past ten years of All Japan Radio and Television CM festival. With the use of data mining capabilities, "AI-CD ß" can extract ideas and themes fulfilling every client's individual campaign needs.

Personalization of User Experience

The expectations of the on-demand entertainment users for rich and engaging personal user experience is ever-growing. One of the leading on-demand entertainment platforms, Netflix, rolled out an artificial intelligence-based workflow management and scheduling application called "Meson," comprised of various "machine learning pipelines" that are capable of creating, training and validating personalization algorithms, to provide personalized recommendations to users. Netflix collaborated with the University of Southern California to develop a new Machine learning algorithms that can compress video for high-quality streaming without degrading image quality called "Dynamic Optimizer." This artificial intelligence technology will address streaming problems in developing nations and mobile device users by optimizing video fluency and definition.

IBM Watson recently collaborated with IRIS. The TV offers a business-to-business service to media companies such as CBS, The Hollywood Reporter, and Hearst Digital Media by tracking and improving the introduction of their customers with their web content. IBM Watson is boosting IRIS.TV company's Machine learning algorithms that can 'learn' from users' search history and recommend similar content. Reportedly a 50% increase in view or retention or a small PDF three months was achieved by the Hollywood reporter with the use of IRIS.TV application.

Search Optimization and Classification

The ability to transform text, audio, and video content into digital copies has led to an explosion of media availability on the Internet, making it difficult for people to find exactly what they're looking for. To optimize the accuracy of search results, advancements are being made in machine learning technology. For example, Google is using artificial intelligence to augment its platform for accurate image searching. People can now simply upload a sample picture to Google Image instead of typing in keywords for their search. The image recognition technology used by Google image Will automatically identify and manage features of the uploaded user image and provide search results with similar pictures. Google is also using artificial intelligence technology in advertisement positioning across the platform. For example, a pet food ad will only appear on the pet-related website, but a chicken wings advertisement will not appear on a site targeted to vegetarians.

The company Vintage Cloud has partnered with artificial intelligence-based startup called "ClarifAI" to develop a film digitalization platform. With the use of computer vision API provided by ClarifAI, Vintage Cloud succeeded in burgeoning the speed of movie content classification and categorization.

A visual assets management platform integrated with machine learning algorithms has been developed by a company called "Zorroa." This platform enables users to search for specific content within large databases called an "Analysis Pipeline." The database contains processors that can tag each visual asset uniquely and Machine learning algorithms that have been 'trained' to identify specific components of the visual data. This visual content is then organized and cataloged to deliver high-quality search results.

Artificial Intelligence vs. Machine Learning

Machine learning in its native form is simply a segment of Artificial Intelligence, as described by pioneering machine learning expert, Tom Mitchell: "Machine learning is the study of computer algorithms that enable computer programs to enhance automatically through experience." Machine learning has been deemed as a way of achieving AI and is based on working with a range of data sets to examine and compare data in order to discover prevalent patterns and discover insights. For example, you could train a machine learning model with a variety of music of your choice along with some corresponding audio statistics, such as tempo or genre. Based on the type of machine learning algorithm used, the model would be able to automate and create a recommendation system providing you suggestions of songs that you could enjoy. This is a very high-level understanding of the model employed by "Netflix," "Spotify," and "iTunes."

On the other hand, artificial intelligence boasts a much wider scope of technological advancements. According to a renowned computer scientist, Andrew Moore from Carnegie Mellon University, "Artificial intelligence is the science and engineering of making computers behave in ways that, until recently, we thought required human intelligence." That's an excellent definition of AI in one phrase, but it still demonstrates how wide and obscure the area is. Decades ago, a machine that could play chess was regarded as a form of AI, since it was considered that only a human brain could exercise gaming theory and strategies. The game of chess today is considered to be dull and antique, primarily because it is easily accessible on every computer operating system. Zachary Lipton, a researcher at Carnegie Mellon University, clarified that AI "is aspirational, a moving target based on those capabilities that humans possess but which machines do not." It even entails a wide variety of technological advancements in our world today. One of them is "machine learning." For example, Deep Blue, the AI that won the world chess championship in 1997, was driven by the decision tree search algorithms to assess millions of steps for its every move.

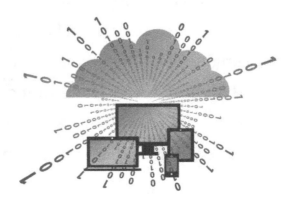

Our present understanding of AI is symbolized by interactive devices like "Google Home," "Apple Siri" and "Amazon Alexa," as well as by "Netflix," "Amazon" and "YouTube" which provide powerful machine learning video recommendation technologies. In our daily life, these advances in technology become increasingly crucial. Indeed, they are smart helpers that are strengthening our human abilities and professional skills, making us increasingly productive. As opposed to machine learning, AI can be considered a moving target, with a definition that changes according to the technological advances that it drives.

Chapter 4:Big Data Analytics 101

In 2001, Gartner defined Big data as "Data that contains greater variety arriving in increasing volumes and with ever-higher velocity." This led to the formulation of the "three V's." Big data refers to an avalanche of structured and unstructured data that is endlessly flooding and from a variety of endless data sources. These data sets are too large to be analyzed with traditional analytical tools and technologies but have a plethora of valuable insights hiding underneath.

The "Vs" of Big data

Volume – To be classified as big data, the volume of the given data set must be substantially larger than traditional data sets. These data sets are primarily composed of unstructured data with limited structured and semi-structured data. The unstructured data or the data with unknown value can be collected from input sources such as webpages, search history, mobile applications, and social media platforms. The size and customer base of the company is usually proportional to the volume of the data acquired by the company.

Velocity – The speed at which data can be gathered and acted upon the first to the velocity of big data. Companies are increasingly using a combination of on-premise and cloud-based servers to increase the speed of their data collection. The modern-day "Smart Products and Devices" require real-time access to consumer data, in order to be able to provide them a more engaging and enhanced user experience.

Variety – Traditionally, a data set would contain majority of structured data with low volume of unstructured and semi-structured data, but the advent of big data has given rise to new unstructured data types such as video, text, audio that require sophisticated tools and technologies to clean and process these data types to extract meaningful insights from them.

Veracity – Another "V" that must be considered for big data analysis is veracity. This refers to the "trustworthiness or the quality" of the data. For example, social media platforms like "Facebook" and "Twitter" with blogs and posts containing a hashtag, acronyms and all kinds of typing errors can significantly reduce the reliability and accuracy of the data sets.

Value – Data has evolved as a currency of its own with intrinsic value. Just like traditional monetary currencies, the ultimate value of the big data is directly proportional to the insight gathered from it.

History of Big Data

The origin of large volumes of data can be traced back to the 1960s and 1970s when the Third Industrial Revolution had just started to kick in, and the development of relational databases had begun along with the construction of data centers. But the concept of big data has recently taken center stage primarily since the availability of free search engines like Google and Yahoo, free online entertainment services like YouTube and social media platforms like Facebook. In 2005, businesses started to recognize the incredible amount of user data being generated through these platforms and services. In the same year, an open-source framework called "Hadoop," was developed to gather and analyze these large data dumps available to the companies. During the same period non-relational or distributed database called "NoSQL" started to gain popularity due to its ability to store and extract unstructured data. "Hadoop" made it possible for the companies to work with big data with high ease and at a relatively low cost.

Today with the rise of cutting-edge technology not only humans but machines also generating data. The smart device technologies like "Internet of things" (IoT) and "Internet of systems" (IoS) have skyrocketed the volume of big data. Our everyday household objects and smart devices are connected to the Internet and able to track and record our usage patterns as well as our interactions with these products and feeds all this

data directly into the big data. The advent of machine learning technology has further increased the volume of data generated on a daily basis. It is estimated that by 2020, "1.7 MB of data will be generated per second per person." As the big data will continue to grow, it usability still has many
horizons to cross.

Importance of Big Data

To gain reliable and trustworthy information from a data set, it is very important to have a complete data set that has been made possible with the use of big data technology. The more data we have, the more information and details can be extracted out of it. To gain a 360 view of a problem, and its underlying solutions, the future of big data is very promising. Here are some examples of the use of big data:

Product development – Large and small e-commerce businesses are increasingly relying upon big data to understand customer demands and expectations. Companies can develop predictive models to launch new products and services by using primary characteristics of their past and existing products and services and generating a model describing the relationship of those characteristics with the commercial success of those products and services. For example, a leading fast manufacturing commercial goods company "Procter & Gamble," extensively uses big data gathered from the social media websites, test markets and focus groups in preparation for their new product launch.

Predictive maintenance – In order to besides leave project potential mechanical and equipment failures, a large volume of unstructured data such as error messages, log entries and normal temperature of the machine must be analyzed along with available structured data such as make and model of the equipment and year of manufacturing. By analyzing this big data set using the required analytical tools, companies can extend the shelf life of their equipment by preparing for scheduled maintenance ahead of time and predicting future occurrences of potential mechanical failures.

Customer experience – The smart customer is aware of all of the technological advancements and is loyal only to the most engaging and enhanced user experience available. This has triggered a race among the companies to provide unique customer experiences analyzing the data gathered from customers' interactions with the company's products and services. Providing personalized recommendations and offers to reduce customer churn rate and effectively kind words prospective leads into paying customers.

Fraud and compliance – Big data helps in identifying the data patterns and assessing historical trends from previous fraudulent transactions to effectively detect and prevent potentially fraudulent transactions. Banks, financial institutions, and online payment services like "PayPal" are continually monitoring and gathering customer transaction data in an effort to prevent fraud.

Operational efficiency – With the help of big data predictive analysis, companies can learn and anticipate future demand and product trends by analyzing production capacity, customer feedback, and data pertaining to top selling items and product returns to improve decision-making and produce products that are in line with the current market trends.

Machine learning – For a machine to be able to learn and train on its own, it requires a humongous volume of data i.e., big data. A solid training set containing structured, semi-structured and unstructured data, will help the machine to develop a multidimensional view of the real world and the problem it is engineered to resolve. (Details on machine learning will be provided later in this book.)

Drive innovation – By studying and understanding the relationships between humans and their electronic devices as well as the manufacturers of these devices, companies can develop improved and innovative products by examining current product trends and meeting customer expectations.

"The importance of big data doesn't revolve around how much data you have, but what you do with it. You can take data from any source and analyze it to find answers that enable 1) cost reductions, 2) time reductions, 3) new product development and optimized offerings, and 4) smart decision making."
- SAS

The Functioning of Big Data

There are three important actions required to gain insights from big data:

Integration – The traditional data integration methods such as ETL (Extract, Transform, Load) are incapable of collating data from a wide variety of unrelated sources and applications that are you at the heart of big data. Advanced tools and technologies are required to analyze big data sets that are exponentially larger than traditional data sets. By integrating big data from these disparate sources, companies are able to analyze and extract valuable insight to grow and maintain their businesses.

Management – Big data management can be defined as "the organization, administration, and governance of large volumes of both structured and unstructured data." Big data requires efficient and cheap storage, which can be accomplished using servers that are on premise, cloud-based, or a combination of both. Companies are able to seamlessly access required data from anywhere across the world and then processing these data using required processing engines on an as-needed basis. The goal is to make sure the quality of the data is high-level and can be accessed easily by needed tools and applications. Big data gathered from all kinds of Dale sources, including social media platforms, search engine history, and call logs. The big data usually contain large sets of unstructured data and the semi-structured data which are stored in a variety of formats. To be able to process and store this complicated data, companies require more powerful and advanced data management software beyond the traditional relational databases and data warehouse platforms.

New platforms are available in the market that are capable of combining big data with the traditional data warehouse systems in a "logical data warehousing architecture." As part of this effort, companies are required to make decisions on what data must be secured for regulatory purposes and compliance, what data must be kept for future analytical purposes and what data has no future use and can be disposed of. This process is called "data classification," which allows rapid and efficient analysis of the subset of data to be included in an immediate decision-making process of the company.

Analysis – Once the big data has been collected and is easily accessible, it can be analyzed using an advance analytical tools and technologies. This analysis will provide valuable insight and actionable information. Big data can be explored to make new discoveries and develop data models using artificial intelligence and machine learning algorithms.

Big Data Analytics

The terms of big data and big data analytics are often used interchangeably going to the fact that the inherent purpose of big data is to be analyzed. "Big data analytics" can be defined as a set of qualitative and quantitative methods that can be employed to examine a large amount of unstructured, structured and semi-structured data to discover data patterns and valuable hidden insights. Big data analytics is the science of analyzing big data to collect metrics, key performance indicators and Data trends that can be easily lost in the flood of raw data, buy using machine learning algorithms and automated analytical techniques. The different steps involved in "big data analysis" are:

Gathering Data Requirements – It is important to understand what information or data needs to be gathered to meet the business objective and goals. Data organization is also very critical for efficient and accurate data analysis. Some of the categories in which the data can be organized are gender, age, demographics, location, ethnicity, and income. A decision must also be made on the required data types (qualitative and quantitative) and data values (can be numerical or alphanumerical) to be used for the analysis.

Gathering Data – Raw data can be collected from disparate sources such as social media platforms, computers, cameras, other software applications, company websites, and even third-party data providers. The big data analysis inherently requires large volumes of data, the majority of which is unstructured with a limited amount of structured and semi-structured data.

Data organization and categorization – Depending on the company's infrastructure Data organization could be done on a simple Excel spreadsheet or using and man tools and applications that are capable of processing statistical data. Data must be organized and categorized based on data requirements collected in step one of the big data analysis process.

Cleaning the data – To perform the big data analysis sufficiently and rapidly, it is very important to make sure the data set is void of any redundancy and errors. Only a complete data set fulfilling the Data requirements must proceed to the final analysis step. Preprocessing of data is required to make sure the only high-quality data is being analyzed, and company resources are being put to good use.

"Big data is high-volume, and high-velocity and/or high-variety information assets that demand cost-effective, innovative forms of information processing that enable enhanced insight, decision making, and process automation."

- Gartner

Analyzing the data – Depending on the insight that is expected to be achieved by the completion of the analysis, any of the following four different types of big data analytics approach can be adopted:

Predictive analysis – This type of analysis is done to generate forecasts and predictions for future plans of the company. By the completion of a predictive analysis on company's big data, the future state of the company can be more precisely predicted and derived from the current state of the company. The business executives are keenly interested in this analysis to make sure the day-to-day company operations are in line with the future vision of the company. For example, to deploy advanced analytical tools and applications in the sales division of a company, the first step is to analyze the leading source of data. Once believes source analysis has been completed the type and number of communication channels for the sales team must be analyzed. This is followed by the use of machine learning algorithms on customer data to gain insight into how the existing customer base is interacting with the company's products or services. This predictive analysis will conclude with the deployment of artificial intelligence-based tools to skyrocket the company's sales.

Prescriptive analysis – Analysis that is carried out by primarily focusing on the business rules and recommendations to generate a selective analytical path as prescribed by the industry standards to boost company performance. The goal of this analysis is to understand the intricacies of various departments of the organization and what measures should be taken by the company to be able to gain insights from its customer data by using the prescribed analytical pathway. This allows the company to embrace domain specificity and conciseness by providing a sharp focus on its existing and future big data analytics process.

Descriptive analysis – All the incoming data received and stored by the company can be analyzed to produce insightful descriptions on the basis of the results obtained. The goal of this analysis is to identify data patterns and current market trends that can be adopted by the company to grow its business. For example, credit card companies often require risk assessment results on all prospective customers, to be able to make predictions on the likelihood of the customer failing to make their credit payments and make a decision whether the customer should be approved for the credit or not. This risk assessment it's primarily based on the customer's credit history but also takes into account other influencing factors including remarks from other financial institutions that the customer had approached for credit, customer income and financial performance as well as their digital footprint and social media profile.

Diagnostic analysis – As the name suggests this type of analysis is done to "diagnose" or understand why a certain event unfolded and how that event can be prevented from occurring in the future or replicated if needed. For example, web marketing strategies and campaigns often employ social media platforms to get publicity and increase their goodwill. Not all campaigns are as successful as expected; therefore, learning from failed campaigns is just as important if not more. Companies can run diagnostic analysis on their campaign by collecting data pertaining to the "social media mentions" of the campaign, number of campaign page views, the average amount of time spent on the campaign page by an individual, number of social media fans and followers of the campaign, online reviews and other related metrics to understand why the campaign failed and how future campaigns can be made more effective.

The big data analysis can be conducted using one or more of the tools listed below:

- **Hadoop** – Open source data framework.
- **Python** – Programming language widely used for machine learning.
- **SAS** – Advanced analytical tool used primarily for big data analysis.
- **Tableau** – Artificial intelligence-based tool used primarily for data visualization.
- **SQL** – Programming language used to extract data from relational databases.

- **Splunk** – Analytical tool used to categorize machine-generated data
- **R-programming** – the Programming language used primarily for statistical computing.

Chapter 5:Web Marketing

Over 2.6 billion and counting active social media users include customers and potential customers for every company out there. The race is on to create more effective marketing and social media strategies, powered by artificial intelligence technology, aimed at providing enhanced customer experience to turn prospective customers into raving fans. The process of sifting through and analyzing a massive amount of data has not only become feasible, but it's actually easy now. The ability to bridge artificial intelligence marketing solutions have supplemented the gap between execution and data science.

Artificial intelligence marketing or AI marketing can be defined as a method of you using artificial intelligence consonants like machine learning on available customer data to anticipate customer's needs and expectations while significantly improving the customer's journey. Marketers are able to boost their campaign performance and return on investment read a little to no extra effort, in the light of big data insights provided by artificial intelligence marketing solutions. The key elements that make AI marketing as powerful are:

- Big data - A marketing company's ability to aggregate and segment colossal dump of data with minimal manual work is referred to as Big Data. The marketer can then leverage the desired medium to ensure the appropriate message is being delivered to the target audience at the right time.
- Machine learning - Machine learning platforms enable marketers to identify trends or common occurrences and gather effective insights and responses, thereby deciphering the root cause and probability of recurring events.
- Intuitive platform – Super fast and easy to operate applications are integral to AI marketing. Artificial intelligence technology is capable of interpreting emotions and communicating like a

human, allowing AI-based platforms to understand open form content like email responses and social media.

Here are some of the most popular and promising AI marketing applications dominating the space:

Lead Generation

The artificial intelligence technology, in combination with machine learning, can not only forecast sales and predict stocks, but it can also create better leads and sales. To grow the business, companies need to generate new and better leads and convert them into sales. AI-powered tools can generate relevant customer information in real-time and account for shifts in current market trends. It can isolate prospective customers who are more likely to make a purchase from customers the only browsing or inquiring. For example, an AI-powered system called "CaliberMind" can analyze human language from social media platforms and marketing automation to generate buyer personas and recommend types of communication that could be more effective. Recently Harley-Davidson experimented with artificial intelligence at one of their New York City branches, which resulted in two times more sales over that weekend than the best sales weekend the company ever had before.

The artificial intelligent technology is not only capable of assessing which advertisements are more effective but also specific parts of an ad that resulted in higher impact. With a few modifications to the target areas, the companies can make them and social media sites much more impactful. This, in turn, helps in successful lead generation from social media campaigns. For example, an AI-based system called "Netra" can analyze visual content such as logos and demographic interests from social media ads to understand users' interests and generate better leads.

Some of the artificial intelligence basis systems that can generate new leads for the company are:

"Node" – It assesses connections between people, products, and companies to discover individuals that might become customers.

"Siftrock" – This software can be integrated with companies existing marketing automation software to generate new leads from customer data points such as email signatures and out of office replies.

"LinkedIn Sales Navigator tool" – The LinkedIn system uses algorithms to identify new leads and customize lead recommendations for individual user's unique profile.

A Harvard business review research study concluded that businesses with artificial intelligence technology Incorporated in their sales systems had a 50% increase in lead generation. Certain artificial intelligence technology-based systems can help get more out of the existing leads and close sales. For example, "eRelevance Corporation" can target existing customers with High conversion marketing campaigns and use predictive data analysis to generate more repeat business. "OneSpot" can maximize visitor engagement by generating personalized website content. Increase engagement, in turn, results in higher conversion rates.

MarketingFunnel

A description of customer's journey from the initial stage of awareness where they learn about the business to the final stage of making a purchase is referred to as the "marketing funnel."The marketing funnel starts with lead generation and maps the conversion of the potential customer into a product buyer. There are five stages in the marketing funnel: awareness, interest, evaluation, commitment and sale.

This concept is applicable to online sales as well as customer interactions with brick and mortar stores. The funnel allows measurability and brings visibility to every stage of customer interaction so companies can modify their marketing strategies and social media campaigns to achieve a higher conversion rate. A successful journey requires each of the five phases of the funnel to work as a unified whole. The marketing funnel framework has been derived from other "hierarchy of effects" model-like "AIDA" which stands for "Attention, Interest, Desire, Action" and proposes that customers move through a series of stages before eventually buying a product or service.

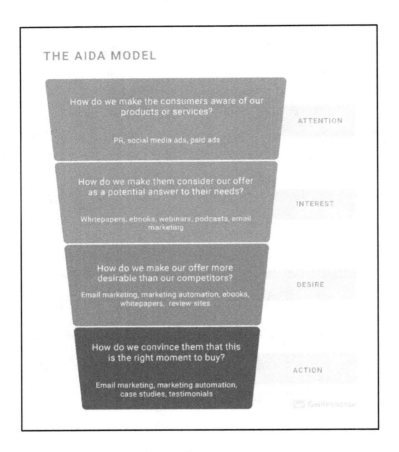

THE AIDA MODEL

How do we make the consumers aware of our products or services?

ATTENTION

PR, social media ads, paid ads

How do we make them consider our offer as a potential answer to their needs?

INTEREST

Whitepapers, ebooks, webinars, podcasts, email marketing

How do we make our offer more desirable than our competitors?

DESIRE

Email marketing, marketing automation, ebooks, whitepapers, review sites

How do we convince them that this is the right moment to buy?

ACTION

Email marketing, marketing automation, case studies, testimonials

A research study done by Accenture estimated that Business owners could save up to 54% of their daily by adopting artificial intelligence technology into their marketing strategies. Unlike sales professionals who rely on their experience and instincts to decide which products to recommend to their clients, AI empowers the sales professionals to base their decisions on customer insights, resulting in a higher conversion rate. Sales professionals can spend more time closing sales as well as building and maintaining customer relationships rather than spending time on tasks like lead generation, lead management and other mundane tasks that can be automated using artificial intelligence technology. This, in turn, increases customer loyalty and brings in repeat business. By incorporating artificial intelligence in their business, companies can get the boost they need to push the prospects through the marketing funnel much faster.

Artificial intelligence-based tools like "GetResponse Autofunnel" help companies identify the best steps to be included in their marketing funnel by removing the guesswork and offering predesigned templates and funnel scenarios. Traditionally companies would have to create their own marketing funnel by running social media ads, setting up autoresponder email sequences, developing landing pages, setting up exit intent forms and creating upsell or cart abandonment offers and then connecting all these elements and more via integrations and plug-ins. The use of "GetResponse Autofunnel" companies can get all these elements in one single platform and save time and money on separate tools supporting separate elements like email autoresponders, landing page builder and social media adds creator and so on. This AI-based tool has built-in payment processing and tracking functionalities which allows companies to sell and measure their sales results using an intuitive Dashboard.

Smart Searches

Only a decade ago if you type in "women's flip flops" on Nike.com, the probability of you finding what you were looking for would be next to zero. But today's search engines are not only accurate but also much faster. This upgrade has largely been brought on by innovations like "semantic search" and "natural language processing" that enable search engines to identify links between products and provide relevant search results, recommend similar items and auto-correct typing errors. The artificial intelligence technology and big data solutions are able to rapidly analyze user search patterns and identify key areas that the marketing companies should focus on.

In 2015, Google introduced the first AI-based search algorithm called "RankBrain." Following Google's lead other major e-commerce websites including Amazon has incorporated artificial intelligence into their search engines to offer smart search experience for their customers, who are able to find desired products even when they don't know exactly what they're looking for. Even small e-commerce stores have access to Smart search technologies like "Elasticsearch." The data-as-a-service companies like "Indix" allow companies to learn from other larger data sources to train their own product search models.

Recommendation Engines

Recommendation engines have quickly evolved into fan favorites and are loved by the customers just as much as the marketing companies. "Apple Music" already knows your taste in music better than your partner, and Amazon always presents you with a list of products that you might actually be interested in buying. This kind of discovery aide that is able to sift through millions of available options and hone in on an individual's need is proving indispensable for large companies with huge physical and digital inventories.

In 1998, Swedish computational linguist, Jussi Karlgren, explored the practice of clustering customer behaviors to predict future behaviors in his report titled "Digital bookshelves." The same here, Amazon implemented collaborative filtering to generate recommendations for their customers. The gathering and analysis of consumer data paired with individual profile information and demographics, by the artificial intelligence-based systems allow the system to continually learn and adapt based on consumer activities such as likes and dislikes on the products in real-time. For example, the company "Sky" has implemented an artificial intelligence-based model that is capable of recommending content according to the viewer's mode. The smart customer is looking for such an enhanced experience not only from their Music and on-demand entertainment suppliers but also from all other e-commerce websites.

Product Categorization and Pricing

E-commerce businesses and marketing companies have increasingly adopted artificial intelligence in their process of categorization and tagging of the inventory. The Marketing companies are required to deal with awful data just as much if not more than amazingly organized clean data. This bag of positive and negative examples serves as training resources for AI-based classification tools. For example, different detailers can have different descriptions for the same product such as sneakers, basketball shoe, trainers or Jordan's but the AI algorithm can identify that these are all the same products and tag them accordingly. Or if the data set is missing the primary keyword like skirts or shirts, the artificial intelligence algorithm can identify and classify the item or product as skirts or shirts based solely on the surrounding context.

We are familiar with the seasonal rate changes of the hotel rooms, but with the advent of artificial intelligence, product prices can be optimized to meet the demand with a whole new level of precision. The machine learning algorithms are being used for dynamic pricing by analyzing customer's data patterns and making near accurate predictions of what they are willing to pay for that particular product as well as their receptiveness to special offers. This empowers businesses to target their consumers with high precision and calculated whether or not a discount is needed to confirm the sale. Dynamic pricing also allows businesses to compare their product pricing with the market leaders and competitors and adjust their prices accordingly to pull in the sale. For example, Airbnb has developed its own dynamic pricing system which provides 'Price Tips' to the property owners to help them determine the best possible listing price for their property. The system takes into account a variety of influencing factors such as geographical location, local events, property pictures, property reviews, listing features, and most importantly, the booking timings and the market demand. The final decision of the property owner to follow or ignore the provided 'price tips' and the success of the listing are also monitored by the system which will then process the results and adjust its algorithm accordingly.

Augmented Reality

Computers are now capable of "seeing" the world through digital images and videos and develop a high-level understanding of what is out there. In order to achieve true 'Computer vision' artificial intelligence, machine learning algorithms, and massive Data sets are required to train the machine on successful recognition and identification of a variety of objects. The concept of augmented reality is driven by computer vision technology. For realistic and accurate overlay of augmented reality on the physical world, computers need to be able to detect and identify the real world with greater accuracy. To enable augmented reality-based advertising that integrates read people's surroundings realistically but without being intrusive has the potential to open new doors for marketing techniques such as interactive shopping, product insights, and offers, and business information.

Home improvement and furniture companies like IKEA, Lowe's, Home Depot have already successfully deployed augmented reality in their marketing strategies. And 2013 Home Depot integrated augmented reality within their mobile application that allowed customers to view how furniture, doors, vanity units, and faucets would look like in their home. In 2015, Home Depot launched "Project Color," an augmented reality-based application that allows users to visualize how different paint colors would actually look on their walls. Lowe's has developed an artificial intelligence-based application called "Measured," which allows customers to measure an object or distance using augmented reality. Lowe's and IKEA also have similar augmented reality based functionalities as Home Depot within their mobile application.

 The cosmetic industry has also jumped on the augmented reality bandwagon by introducing augmented reality-based applications to engage consumers and drive down return purchases. Some of the leading cosmetic brands like Sephora, L'Oreal, Estee Lauder and Lancôme have deployed augmented reality within their mobile applications that allow consumers to virtually try on cosmetic products like lipsticks or eyeliners or nail varnish on their virtual self-generated by the augmented reality functionality of the application. Consumers are able to get a feel of the product on their own face without needing to visit the store. They are also able to try on a variety of products within minutes at their own leisure personalize product recommendations based on their purchase history and search criteria. Users can also carry out a full makeover right from the comfort of their home while learning about the products they need as well as how to apply them.

Sales and Marketing Forecast

One of the most straightforward artificial intelligence applications in marketing is in the development of sales and marketing forecasting models. The high volume of quantifiable data such as clicks, purchases, email responses, and time spent on the webpage serve as training resources for the machine learning algorithms. Some of the leading business intelligence and production companies in the market are Sisense, Rapidminer, and Birst. Marketing companies are continuously upgrading their marketing efforts, and with the help of AI and machine learning, they can predict the success of their marketing initiatives or email campaigns. Artificial intelligence technology can analyze past sales data, economic trends, as well as industrywide comparisons to predict short and long-term sales performance and forecast sales outcomes. The sales forecasts model aid in the estimation of product demand and to help companies manage their production to optimize sales.

Speech Recognition

Due to the advancements made in the speech recognition technology over the past few years, it has become the talk of the town in the marketing Industry. 2016 brought a flood of incredible voice-driven and chat-based devices or interfaces into the world of marketing. Amazon Echo has successfully turned the Internet of things technology into in reality buy enabling customers to make purchases would simple voice commands. Customers can order Pizza or an Uber car by simply speaking to the device. Google and Apple have launched their own personal assistant home devices called "Google Home" and "Apple HomePod," respectively. Another example is "Baidu's Duer," which is a Chatbot that enables customers to order products within its interface. Facebook messenger has also targeted the online to the offline marketing strategy of "chat-based purchases," that allows customers to place orders via chat alone.

And 2017, Google reported that their speech recognition accuracy had reached a 95% threshold only to be trumped by and that claimed to have reached 97% and is aiming for 99% accuracy with their speech recognition technology. The travel company called "Trainline" launched an artificial intelligence-based voice application for the Google Assistant and is considered the UK's most advanced voice artificial intelligence technology with 12 levels of conversation depth. The learns and trains itself with every iteration to become more accurate with increased use by the commuters.

Programmatic Advertisement Targeting

With the introduction of artificial intelligence technology bidding on and targeting program based advertisements has become significantly more efficient. Programmatic advertising can be defined as "the automated process of buying and selling ad inventory to an exchange which connects advertisers to publishers." To allow real-time bidding for inventory across social media channels and mobile devices as well as television, artificial intelligence technology is used. This also goes back to predictive analysis and the ability to model data that could previously only be determined retroactively. Artificial intelligence is able to assist the best time of the day to serve a particular ad, the probability of an ad turning into sales, the receptiveness of the user and the likelihood of engagement with the ad.

Programmatic companies have the ability to gather and analyze visiting customers' data and behaviors to optimize real-time campaigns and to target the audience more precisely. Programmatic media buying includes the use of "demand-side platforms" (to facilitate the process of buying ad inventory on the open market) and "data management platforms" (to provide the marketing company able to reach their target audience). In order to empower the marketing rep to make informed decisions regarding their prospective customers, the data management platforms are designed to collect and analyze big volume of website "cookie data." For example, search engine marketing (SEM) advertising practiced by channels like Facebook, Twitter, and Google. To efficiently manage huge inventory of the website and application viewers, programmatic ads provide a significant edge over competitors. Google and Facebook serve as the gold standard for efficient and effective advertising and are geared to words providing a user-friendly platform that will allow non-technical marketing companies to start, run and measure their initiatives and campaigns online.

Visual Search and Image Recognition

Leaps and bounds of the advancements in artificial intelligence-based image recognition and analysis technology have resulted in uncanny visual search functionalities. With the introduction of technology like Google Lens and platforms like Pinterest, people can now find results that are visually similar to one another using the visual search functionality. The visual search works in the same way as traditional text-based searches that display results on a similar topic. Major retailers and marketing companies are increasingly using the visual search to offer an enhanced and more engaging customer experience. Visual search can be used to improve merchandising and provide product recommendations based on the style of the product instead of consumer's past behavior or purchases.

Major investments have been made by Target and Asos in the visual search technology development for their e-commerce website. In 2017, Target announced a partnership with interest that allows integration of Pinterest's visual search application called "Pinterest lens" into Target's mobile application. As a result, shoppers can take a picture of products that they would like to purchase while they are out and about and find similar items on Target's e-commerce site. Similarly, the visual search application launched by Asos called "Asos' Style Match" allows shoppers to snap a photo or upload an image on Asos website or application and search their product catalogue for similar items. These tools attract shoppers to retailers for items that they might come across in a magazine or while out and about by helping them to shop for the ideal product even if they do not know what the product is.

Image recognition has tremendously helped marketing companies to gain an edge on social media by allowing them to find a variety of uses of their brand logos and products in keeping up with the visual trends. This phenomenon is also called "visual social listening" and allows companies to identify and understand where and how customers are interacting with their brand, logo, and product even when the company is not referred directly by its name.

Intelligent Email Content Curation

From a 2016 study done by a demand metric, it can be concluded that 80% of marketing companies claim that personalize content is more effective in tapping prospective customers than generic content. The marketing team spends significant time in and scheduling weekly emails to the company's wide base of customer segments. Delivering a personalized email to every single customer is nothing short of a Herculean task, even with smart subscriber segmentation. Enters artificial intelligence technology! The advanced AI algorithms are capable of mapping a user's interaction with the website and email browsing data to gather insight on every user's engagement and experience with the company's online content. This information then triggers the algorithm to generate highly individualistic and personalized emails for all the customers with the identification of the hyper contextual content.

These dynamic, personalized emails can be composed based on an individual's wish list, previous, time spent on a particular webpage, blogs and articles read in the past, interest of similar visitors, prior interactions with the company's emails and the most popular content at the time. The analysis of consumer's reading patterns and areas of interest can be used to generate specific content recommendations in relevance to the individual and send personal curated emails to all of their consumers.

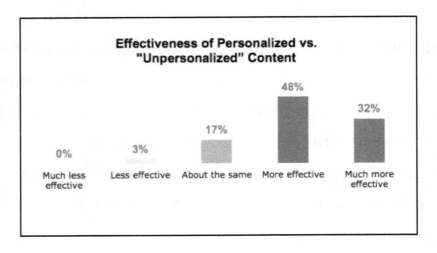

Real-Time Customer Service

One of the fundamental requirements of the customer in a good online experience is quick response and resolution of their problems. The artificial intelligence technology can deliver that seamless experience to the customer in real-time through the AI Chatbots, which can easily give customers the impression that they are speaking with a human customer service representative. Chatbots can easily answer basic customer inquiries, track and fulfill orders, and addressed simple issues; all along using familiar terms to seem more 'human-like.' For example, "Facebook Messenger" has recently been integrated with the Chatbot functionality for the company's official Facebook pages to provide enhanced real-time customer service to other businesses. Chatbots are extremely useful in reducing call wait times for customers having complex issues and are available 24/7 without fatigue.

Conclusion

Thank you for making it through to the end of ***Machine Learning for Beginners:*** *Step-by-Step Guide to Machine Learning, a Beginners Approach to Artificial Intelligence, Big Data, Basic Python Algorithms, and Techniques for Business (Practical Examples)*, let's hope it was informative and able to provide you with all of the tools you need to achieve your goals whatever they may be.

The next step is to make the greatest use of your fresh discovered wisdom on today's cutting-edge techniques that have produced the powerhouse, the Silicon Valley. Today machine learning and artificial intelligence have created advanced machines that can study human behavior and activity to recognize fundamental human behavior patterns and predict exactly what products and services customers are interested in. Businesses with an eye on the future are gradually becoming technology companies, under the façade of their intended business model. Contemporary businesses can readily influence Today's intelligent and savvy clients with a whimsical edge that offer distinctive, rich, and engaging experiences to consumers. Traditional companies are becoming increasingly challenged to maintain their clients without embracing one or more of the cutting-edge technology described in this book.

With an awareness of how much is at risk for your company and how you can position yourself not only to maintain current clients but also to interest more potential clients who will eventually be transformed into a paying customer, you are ready to put your company to greater heights. Start with one step at the moment and comprehend the present position and difficulties of your business, then use your company's strength of artificial intelligence, machine learning, and big data analytics to improve human skills without undermining human intelligence and generating new high-paying and rewarding employment.

Finally, if you found this book useful in any way, a review on Amazon is always appreciated!

www.ingramcontent.com/pod-product-compliance
Lightning Source LLC
Chambersburg PA
CBHW071119050326
40690CB00008B/1270